BOOK **1**

Expressions

Meaningful English Communication

David Nunan

HEINLE & HEINLE

THOMSON LEARNING

Australia · Canada · Mexico · Singapore · Spain · United Kingdom · United States

HEINLE & HEINLE

TM

THOMSON LEARNING

Editorial Director: Nancy Leonhardt
Production Director: Elise Kaiser
Editorial Manager: Christopher Wenger
Senior Development Editor: Sean Bermingham
Development Editors: Colin Toms, Maria O'Conor
Production Editor: Tan Jin Hock

Senior Marketing Manager: Amy Mabley
Interior/Cover Design: Christopher Hanzie, TYA Inc.
Illustrations: Raketshop Design Studio, Philippines
Cover Images: Photodisc
Composition: TYA Inc.
Printer: Seng Lee Press

For more information, contact Heinle & Heinle Publishers, 20 Park Plaza, Boston, MA 02116 USA. Or you can visit our
Internet site at http://www.heinle.com

UK/EUROPE/MIDDLE EAST:
Thomson Learning
Berkshire House
168-173 High Holborn
London WC1V 7AA
United Kingdom

CANADA:
Nelson/Thomson Learning
1120 Birchmount Road
Toronto, Ontario
Canada M1K 5G4

ASIA (including India):
Thomson Learning
60 Albert Street
#15-01 Albert Complex
Singapore 189969

AUSTRALIA/NEW ZEALAND:
Nelson/Thomson Learning
102 Dodds Street
South Melbourne
Victoria 3205, Australia

LATIN AMERICA:
Thomson Learning
Seneca 53
Colonia Polanco
11560 México, D.F. México

SPAIN:
Paraninfo/Thomson Learning
Calle Magallanes 25
28105 Madrid
España

For permission to use the material from this text or product, contact us in the US by
Tel 1 (800) 730-2214
Fax 1 (800) 730-2215
www.thomsonrights.com

Photo credits: Singapore Tourism Board (page 115), Italy Cultural Institute (page 116).

Every effort has been made to trace all sources of illustrations/photos/information in this book, but if any have been inadvertently
overlooked, the publisher will be pleased to make the necessary arrangements at the first opportunity.

ISBN 0-8384-2240-3

Printed in Singapore
2 3 4 5 6 04 03 02 01

AUTHOR'S ACKNOWLEDGMENTS

As always, in a project of this magnitude, there are many people to thank. First and foremost, I would like to acknowledge and thank Christopher Wenger, ELT Editorial Manager for Asia at Heinle & Heinle/Thomson Learning. It was Chris who first saw the potential of *Expressions* and did more than anyone to bring it to fruition. To Grace Low for her contributions to the Read On sections. To John Chapman for his workbooks. To Colin Toms for his detailed and insightful editing. To Nancy Leonhardt for her faith in this project and in me. To Christopher Hanzie, Stella Tan and the staff at T.Y.A. for their round-the-clock efforts under nearly impossible deadlines.

I am indebted to numerous other folks within Heinle & Heinle: Amy Mabley, John Lowe, Ian Martin, Francisco Lozano, Carmelita Benozatti, Sean Bermingham and Tan Jin Hock who, as always, are a joy to work with. I can't thank you enough for your support.

In addition to the above, I would like to extend my thanks to the following professionals who have offered invaluable comments and suggestions during the development of the series:

• Esperanza Bañuelos	CECATI, Mexico City, Mexico
• Graham Bathgate	ELEC, Tokyo, Japan
• James Boyd	ECC Foreign Language Institute, Osaka, Japan
• Gunther Breaux	Dongduk Women's University, Seoul, Korea
• Robert Burgess	NAVA Language Schools, Bangkok, Thailand
• Connie Chang	ELSI, Taipei, Taiwan
• Clara Inés García Frade	Universidad Militar 'Nueva Granada,' Santafé de Bogotá, Colombia
• Rob Gorton	Kumamoto YMCA, Kumamoto, Japan
• Randall Grev	ELSI, Taipei, Taiwan
• Ross Hackshaw	IAI Girls' Junior & Senior High School, Hakodate, Japan
• Ann-Marie Hadzima	National Taiwan University, Taipei, Taiwan
• Gladys Hong	The Overseas Chinese Institute of Technology, Taichung, Taiwan
• Ching-huei Huang	Oriental Institute of Technology, Taipei, Taiwan
• Ivon Katz	Asian University of Science & Technology, Chonburi, Thailand
• Tim Kirk	Asian University of Science & Technology, Chonburi, Thailand
• Clarice Lamb	ATLAS English Learning Centre, Porto Alegre, Brazil
• Lee Bal-geum	Seul-gi Young-o, Seoul, Korea
• Mike Lee	ELSI, Taipei, Taiwan
• Susan Lee	Seul-gi Young-o, Seoul, Korea
• Jisun Leigh	Hankook English Institute, Seoul, Korea
• Hsin-ying Li	National Taiwan University, Taipei, Taiwan
• Ian Nakamura	Hiroshima Kokusai Gakuin University, Hiroshima, Japan
• Luis Pantoja	Colegio Particular Andino, Huancayo, Peru
• Juan Ramiro Peña	Preparatoria - Benemérita Universidad, Autónoma de Puebla, Puebla, Mexico
• Susanna Philiproussis	Miyazaki International College, Kano, Japan
• Leila Maria Rezende	Solivros, Brasilia, Brazil
• P. Robin Rigby	Hakodate Shirayuri Gakuen Chugakko, Hakodate, Japan
• Lesley D. Riley	Kanazawa Institute of Technology, Ishikawa, Japan
• Mercedes Rossetti	Inglés en Línea S.A., Buenos Aires, Argentina
• Fortino Salazar	Instituto Benjamin Franklin, Mexico City, Mexico
• Beatriz Solina	ARICANA, Rosario, Argentina
• Carolyn Teh	ELSI, Kuala Lumpur, Malaysia
• Daisy William	ELSI, Kuala Lumpur, Malaysia

Scope and sequence

UNIT	Title	Goals	Structures	Listening
1 Page 8	Are you Dr. Lowe?	• Introducing yourself • Practicing greetings • Asking who people are	• Questions and answers with *am/is/are*	• Expressions of introduction
2 Page 16	Is that your family?	• Talking about your family • Asking about families	• *This/that/these/those*	• Family terms
3 Page 24	Do you know Amy?	• Asking about appearance • Describing others	• Questions and answers with *do/does*	• Identifying people
4 Page 32	Where are you from?	• Asking and answering questions about where people are from	• *Is/Are* and *Do/Does*	• Where people are from
5 Page 40	Make yourself at home.	• Welcoming someone • Offering, accepting and refusing	• *Would* and *may*	• Hospitality
6 Page 48	How much is this sweater?	• Asking about and stating prices • Paying for goods	• *How much* and *How many*	• Shopping and prices
7 Page 56	Is there a pool?	• Asking for and identifying locations in a building • Giving directions	• *On/next to/between*	• Hotel facilities/locations
8 Page 64	First, you turn it on.	• Describing procedures • Narrating a sequence	• Sequencing words	• Instructions
9 Page 72	I get up early.	• Describing routines and schedules • Telling time	• Questions with *What + do*	• Time/daily routines
10 Page 80	I'd like a hamburger.	• Ordering food and drink • Asking for additional information	• *Would like* and *Will have*	• Fast food types
11 Page 88	Do you want to see a movie?	• Inviting • Making excuses	• *I'm ___-ing* and *I have to*	• Film genres/ making excuses
12 Page 96	What's the weather like?	• Talking about the weather • Making suggestions	• *Let's* and *going to*	• Weather forecasts
13 Page 104	What can we get him?	• Talking about what people like • Talking about gift giving	• *Let's/How about...?* and *like*	• Hobbies/suggesting gifts
14 Page 112	We should go to the beach.	• Making suggestions • Voicing objections	• *Can* and *should*	• Choosing vacation destinations
15 Page 120	What's she like?	• Describing people and jobs • Using degrees of description	• Adverbs of degree + adjectives	• Jobs and character types
16 Page 128	I lost my cell phone.	• Talking about what you did • Asking about past events	• Simple past	• Talking about your day

Pronunciation	Writing	Reading	Recycling
• Question and statement intonation	• Making a business card	• Changing fashions in names • *Think before you read*	
• Pronouncing *th*	• Writing about your family	• Unusually large families • *Reading actively*	• Possessive adjectives • Asking who people are
• Reduced speech in sounds connecting words	• A letter to a pen pal	• Image consultants • *Inferring vocabulary*	• *Do you...?* • Questions/statements with *is/are*
• Syllable stress	• Filling in a form	• Different places with the same name • *Inferring content*	• Yes/no questions • Introducing yourself
• Pronouncing *c* as /s/ or /k/	• Writing a party invitation	• Visiting people at home • *Scanning*	• Practicing greetings
• Rising intonation for confirmation	• Writing a small ad	• Retro fashions • *Looking for main ideas*	• *It's/they're* • *This/that* • Accepting
• Stress for information	• Writing directions to your classroom	• Services • *Scanning*	• Questions using *where...?* • Imperatives
• Pronouncing /s/ and /sh/	• Writing instructions	• How does it work? • *Identifying reference words*	• Prepositions *in, on* • Giving instructions
• Intonation to transform statements into questions	• Writing a daily schedule	• An unusual daily routine • *Inferring content*	• *What do/does...?* • Narrating a sequence
• Pronouncing /s/ and /z/	• Writing a recipe	• The origins of fast foods • *Scanning*	• *Would* • Offering • Asking about/stating prices
• Intonation to show surprise	• Writing and replying to invitations	• On-line movies • *Identifying reference words*	• *Which* • *Want*
• Stress for information cues	• Writing a weather forecast	• Polar bear clubs • *Skimming*	• *What's...?/it's...* • Time expressions
• Pronouncing *What's* and *what does* in reduced speech	• Writing a thank you note	• Different gift-giving customs • *Reading actively*	• *Let's* • *...ing* for future • Making suggestions
• Pronouncing *can* and *can't*	• Writing a travel brochure	• All-American roads • *Inferring content*	• *Going to* + verb for future • Expressing opinions
• Question and statement intonation	• Describing people in your class	• Suitable business partners • *Inferring vocabulary*	• *What's...like?* • Describing others
• Vowel sounds	• Writing a diary entry	• The Unclaimed Baggage Store • *Identifying reference words*	• Sequencing words • Describing routines • Time expressions

Useful Classroom Expressions

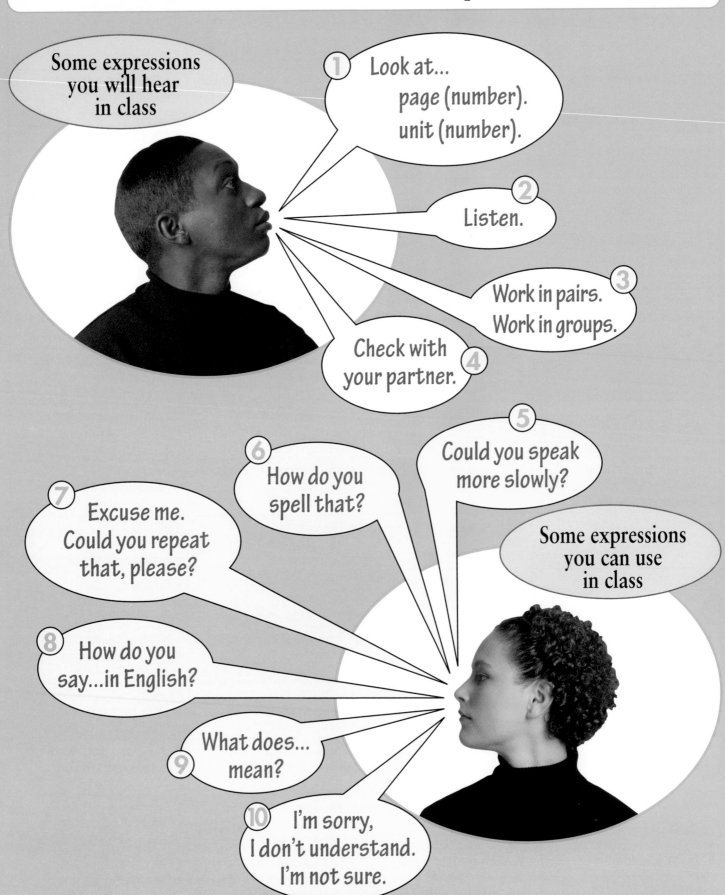

Some expressions you will hear in class

1. Look at...
   page (number).
   unit (number).

2. Listen.

3. Work in pairs.
   Work in groups.

4. Check with your partner.

5. Could you speak more slowly?

6. How do you spell that?

7. Excuse me. Could you repeat that, please?

8. How do you say...in English?

9. What does... mean?

10. I'm sorry, I don't understand. I'm not sure.

Some expressions you can use in class

How do you like to learn?

A Preferences

○ **Which do you like? Put these in order (1–6).**

_____ Speaking	_____ Reading	_____ Grammar
_____ Listening	_____ Writing	_____ Vocabulary

B In class, I like...

○ **Check (✔) the boxes.**

	Not at all	A little	A lot	Not sure
doing role plays				
playing language games				
listening to tapes				
watching videos				
doing pair work				
doing group work				
studying grammar				
listening to the teacher				
writing things down				

C Out of class, I like...

○ **Check (✔) the boxes.**

	Not at all	A little	A lot	Not sure
talking with native English speakers				
watching English TV/movies				
reading English newspapers/books				
studying by myself				
writing letters/a diary in English				
doing homework				
studying from textbooks				
learning English from the Internet				

Check your ideas with a partner. Now you're ready to start *Expressions 1*.

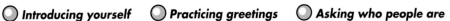

○ **Introducing yourself**   ○ **Practicing greetings**   ○ **Asking who people are**

Are you Dr. Lowe?

1 Get Ready

(A) Look at the people. Write the number of the response in the correct place in the picture.

> 1. Nice to meet you, Rick.
> 2. Yes, I am.
> 3. No, I'm not. I'm Dr. Harris.

(B) Look at these personal titles. Which can be used for men? Which can be used for women? Which can be used for both? Fill in the chart.

Dr.   *Ms.*   *Prof.*

Mrs.   *Mr.*

Men	Women	Both

Speech bubbles in picture: "Are you John West?" "I'm Rick." "Are you Dr. Lowe?" "Dr. LOWE"

2 Start Talking

(A) Look at the conversation and listen.

> Ron: Are you Pat?
> Mary: No, I'm not. I'm Mary.
> Ron: Nice to meet you, Mary. I'm Ron.

Pair work

(B) Practice with a partner. Use your own name. Then change partners and practice again.

3 Listen In

A How many times do you hear each expression? Check (✔) the expressions every time you hear them.

_____ Excuse me.　　　　　_____ Are you...?

_____ Yes, I am.　　　　　_____ No, I'm not.

_____ Nice to meet you.　　_____ What's your name?

B Listen again and number the names you hear (1–4).

_____ Bill　　　　　　　_____ Melinda

_____ Mr. Mendoza　　　_____ Larry Stevens

_____ Mr. Sanders　　　_____ Tina Jones

4 Say It Right

Try this

What's the answer to
Nice to meet you?
Can you remember?

A Listen to the example.

Are you Susan? ↗

No, I'm not. ↘

B Is the intonation rising (↗) or falling (↘)? Listen and mark the intonation.

Excuse me.

Are you Melinda?

Yes?

Yes, I am.

I'm Bill.

Nice to meet you.

C Listen again and practice.

5 Focus In

A Look at the chart.

Questions and answers with *am/is/are*		
Are you Pat?	Yes, I **am**.	No, I**'m** not. I**'m** Peggy./My name**'s** Peggy.
Am I in the right class?	Yes, you **are**.	No, you **aren't**. You**'re** in Class B.
Is he Greg?	Yes, he **is**.	No, he **isn't**. He**'s** Paul./His name**'s** Paul.
Is she Melanie?	Yes, she **is**.	No, she **isn't**. She**'s** Ann./Her name**'s** Ann.
Are they sisters?	Yes, they **are**.	No, they **aren't**. They**'re** friends.

B Fill in the missing information.

1. A: _____ you Pat?
   B: No, _____ not. _____ Lee.

2. A: _____ you from the United States?
   B: No, _____ not. _____ from Canada.

3. A: _____ Lucy your sister?
   B: No, she _____. _____ my friend.

4. A: _____ she Stella?
   B: No, she _____ Yasuko.

C Fill in the blanks in the conversations.

1. A: _____
   B: Hi.
   A: _____
   B: I'm Andy Peters.

2. A: _____
   B: Yes?
   A: _____
   B: No, _____ not. I'm Connie.

6 Talk Some More

Spotlight

Hi is an informal greeting.
How do you do? is a formal greeting.
Hello can be both.

A Number the sentences to make a conversation.

Julie: __6__ Julie Martin.
Julie: _____ Nice to meet you, Kevin.
Kevin: _____ I'm Kevin Tanner.
Julie: _____ Hi.
Kevin: _____ What's your name?
Kevin: __1__ Hello.

B Check your answers.

C Practice the conversation with a partner. Use your own name.

 Pair work

10 Unit 1

7 Work In Pairs (Student A)

A Write the names of four famous people you know in the chart. Say and spell them for your partner. Then ask for your partner's four names and write them down.

You	Your Partner
_____	_____
_____	_____
_____	_____
_____	_____

B Ask your partner for the missing names. Fill in the blanks.

BACK ROW: Lisa Maxwell, _____, Carla Diaz, Roger Walker
FRONT ROW: _____, Eric Simmons, _____

Try this

Ask for the names of your partner's parents.

Your partner's mother: _____

Your partner's father: _____

Work In Pairs (Student B)

Student A: Use page 11

A Write the names of four famous people you know in the chart. Say and spell them for your partner. Then ask for your partner's four names and write them down.

You	Your Partner

B Ask your partner for the missing names. Fill in the blanks.

Number four. What's his name?

Roger Walker.

How do you spell that?

BACK ROW: _____, Edwin Sondhe, _____, Roger Walker

FRONT ROW: Stephen Lee, _____, Susan Chen

Try this

Ask for the names of your partner's parents.

Your partner's mother: _____

Your partner's father: _____

8 Express Yourself

A Ask for your classmates' names. Fill in the list.

Class List

B Cover your list. How many names can you remember?

9 Think About It

In English, when people:

- *want to call a server's attention*
- *want to ask a stranger a question*
- *accidentally step on someone's foot in a crowd*
- *want someone to move out of the way*

they usually say **Excuse me**.
In what situations do you usually say **Excuse me** in your culture?

10 Write About It

A Look at the two business cards.

B Now make your own business card.

Lillian Arroche
International Sales Director

Online Education Inc.
238 Commonwealth Ave.
Boston, MA 02117
Tel: 617-555-7044 Fax: 617-555-7045
E-mail: lilliana@onlineed.com

Dr. Christopher Richie
Department of Humanities

Reading University
Whiteknights
Reading RU5 2BJ, U.K.
Tel: (44) 437 54890 Fax: (44) 437 54894
E-mail: c.richie@internet.com

Baby Names Over the Years

• **Strategy: Think before you read**

• **What's your given name?**
• **Why were you named that?**

How do parents choose the name of their baby?

In the United States, parents often give a baby the name of its father, mother or another family member. Some people just choose a name that's popular at that time. Two hundred years ago, 50% of boy babies in England were named William, John or Thomas, and 50% of girl babies were named Elizabeth, Mary or Anne. Some of these names are still popular, but other names are popular, too. Today, parents sometimes give their babies the names of famous athletes, film stars, characters from literature or TV shows.

Here are some of the most popular baby names over the years:

New York City, 1898
Girls: Mary, Catherine, Margaret, Ann(e), Rose, Marie, Ester, Sarah, Francis, Ida
Boys: John, William, Charles, George, Joseph, Edward, James, Louis, Francis, Samuel

New York City, 1964
Girls: Lisa, Deborah, Mary, Susan, Marie, Elizabeth, Donna, Barbara, Patricia, Ann(e), Theresa
Boys: Michael, John, Robert, David, Steven, Anthony, William, Joseph, Thomas, Christopher, Richard

New York City, 1999
Girls: Emily, Sarah, Brianna, Samantha, Hailey, Ashley, Kaitlyn, Madison, Hannah, Alexis
Boys: Jacob, Michael, Matthew, Nicholas, Christopher, Joshua, Austin, Tyler, Brandon, Joseph

Which names appear on more than one list? Write the names into the chart.

	Boys	Girls
1898		
1964		
1999		

Talk About It

○ What are some popular girls' names and boys' names among people your age?

○ How many names do you have? Do you know what they mean?

○ Do you have a nickname? Why do you have this name?

Review

1 Vocabulary Review

A Fill in the chart with the first names and family names you learned in this unit.

First names	Family names

B How many can you spell from memory?

What's your name?

2 Grammar Review

A Unscramble the sentences and write them correctly.

1. Are/Lowe/Dr./you   *Are you Dr. Lowe?* _____
2. No/not/I'm _____
3. What's/name/your _____
4. meet/to/you/Nice _____
5. spell/do/you/How/that _____

B Fill in the blanks with the correct words.

A: Hi. _____ you Brenda?

B: No, I'_____ not. My name _____ Anna.

A: Hello, Anna. I'_____ Jerry.

B: Hi, Jerry. _____ you in this class?

A: Yes, I _____.

3 Log On

Practice more with the language and topics you studied on the *Expressions* website:

http://expressions.heinle.com

Is that your family?

1 Get Ready

A Look at the people.
Write the numbers of all
the family words possible
for each person in the box,
following the examples.

1. mother
2. father
3. son
4. daughter
5. brother
6. sister
7. husband
8. wife

Lisa **1, 4, 8**
Tim
John **2, 7**
Susan
Katie
Rick

B Look at the family picture, then read the sentences.
Write *T* for true, or *F* for false.

1. _T_ Katie is Tim and Lisa's daughter.
2. ____ Susan is John's mother.
3. ____ Tim is Lisa's husband.
4. ____ Katie is an only child.
5. ____ John is Katie and Rick's father.
6. ____ Rick and Katie are brother and sister.

2 Start Talking

A Look at the conversation and listen.

Hillary: Is that your family?
Lisa: Yes, it is. This is my husband.
Hillary: Are those your children?
Lisa: Yes. This is my son, and this is my daughter.

Pair work **B** Practice with a partner. Then look at the family in Get Ready.
Imagine this is your family. Ask and answer questions about them.

3 Listen In

A Look at the people in the three pictures. Who are the parents? Who are the sons and daughters? Tell your partner.

B Listen and check (✔) the words you hear.

_____ father   _____ mother   _____ husband   _____ wife   _____ children

_____ brother   _____ daughter   _____ sister   _____ son   _____ parents

C Which family is Joe talking about? Listen and check (✔) the correct picture above.

Try this

What are the two different ways of saying *yes* you heard? Can you remember?

4 Say It Right

A Write the number of the picture next to the correct sentence.

_____ This is my daughter.

_____ This is my father.

_____ These are my children.

_____ This is my mother.

B Listen to the conversations and check your answers.

C Listen again. Pay attention to the pronunciation of *this* and *these*. Practice the sentences.

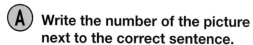

5 Focus In

A Look at the chart.

this/that/these/those		
Is **this** your family?	Yes, it is.	No, it isn't.
Is **that** your husband?	Yes, it is.	No, it isn't.
Are **these** your children?	Yes, they are.	No, they aren't.
Are **those** your sisters?	Yes, they are.	No, they aren't.

B When do we use *this, that, these, those*? Check the spaces.
The first one has been done for you.

	this	that	these	those
Only 1 person or thing	✔			
2+ people or things				
Close to the speaker				
Not close to the speaker				

C Work with a partner. Make up two sentences for each line below.

1. Is _____ your family?
2. Are _____ your children?
3. Is _____ your car?
4. Are _____ your friends?
5. Susan, _____ is my husband.
6. Are _____ your keys?

6 Talk Some More

A Write the words in the correct places.

(I) (you) (have) (do)

Hillary: Do _____ have any
brothers or sisters?

Lisa: Yes, I _____. I _____
a brother and two sisters.
How about you?

Hillary: _____ have two sisters.

Spotlight
*How about you?,
What about you?* **and** *And you?*
have the same meaning.

B Check your answers.

C Practice the conversation with a partner. Use information about your own family.

Work In Pairs

Student A

Student B: Use page 20

A Draw your family tree in the space below. Describe your family to your partner.

I have a father...

My Family Tree

B Imagine you're one of the people in this family.
Answer your partner's questions.

C Ask your partner questions.
Draw your partner's family tree.

Try this

Make up two sentences about your partner's family.

1 _____

2 _____

Work In Pairs   Student B

A Draw your family tree in the space below. Describe your family to your partner.

I have a father...

My Family Tree

B Imagine you're one of the people in this family. Answer your partner's questions.

C Ask your partner questions. Draw your partner's family tree.

Try this

Make up two sentences about your partner's family.

1 _____

2 _____

8 Express Yourself

(A) Ask your classmates questions and write their names.

Find someone who...

	Name
1. has a sister	
2. has two brothers	
3. has a brother and a sister	
4. has more than three brothers or sisters	
5. is an only child	
6. has one child	

Group work

(B) Check your answers.
Then answer these questions.

1. Who has the most brothers in your group?

_____

2. Who has the most sisters in your group?

_____

3. Who has the most children in your group?

_____

Do you have any brothers or sisters?

9 *Think About It*

In some cultures, it is not polite to ask *Are you married?* when meeting for the first time, but in other cultures, it's OK.

• *How about in your culture? When can you usually ask the question* **Are you married?**

10 Write About It

(A) Look at the note and photo.

Here is a photo of my family. They live in Miami, Florida. These are my parents. This is my brother Edward, and my sister Mary.

(B) Go back to your own family tree in Work In Pairs. Then write about your own family.

• Strategy: Reading actively

Read these statements.
Then read the article to mark them *True* or *False*.

	True	False
• The four girls and three boys were born very small.	☐	☐
• The family moved into a new house.	☐	☐
• The family called the president.	☐	☐
• People gave the family many gifts.	☐	☐

At a time when most families are getting smaller, some families are getting much larger.

This is the story of one family.

On November 9, 1997, in Iowa, Bobbi McCaughey had seven babies. The four boys and three girls were born very small. They all stayed in the hospital for many weeks. The president called to congratulate Bobbi and her husband Kenny.

For your information

- *2 babies = twins*
- *3 babies = triplets*
- *4 babies = quadruplets*
- *5 babies = quintuplets*
- *6 babies = sextuplets*
- *7 babies = septuplets*

The family also received a lot of presents. They were given a large new house, a van, diapers, baby care products, food and money. For eight months, volunteers helped the family. Mom and Dad joined with popular singers and made a CD of baby songs. Sales from this CD, called *Sweet Dreams*, have helped the family with the high cost of taking care of seven children.

In 1997, there were born in the United States:
- 104,137 sets of twins
- 6,148 sets of triplets
- 510 sets of quadruplets
- 79 sets of quintuplets or larger numbers of babies

Talk About It

○ Are you a twin or are there any twins in your family?

○ Do you know any twins (or triplets, etc.)? Who?

○ Do you know any stories of famous twins? Who?

1 Vocabulary Review

A Fill in the chart with the family words you learned in this unit.

Men	Women

B How many of these people are there in your family?

2 Grammar Review

A Are these sentences correct? If not, write them correctly in the space.

	Correct	Incorrect	
1. Is these your husband?	☐	✔	*Is this your husband?*
2. Is that your family?	☐	☐	
3. Is those your sisters?	☐	☐	
4. Are you have any brothers?	☐	☐	
5. Do you have any children?	☐	☐	

B Make sentences about your family using the words shown.

1. brother/brothers _____
2. sister/sisters _____
3. married _____
4. children _____

3 Log On

Practice more with the language and topics you studied on the *Expressions* website:

http://expressions.heinle.com

Goals

○ Asking about appearance   ○ Describing others

Do you know Amy?

 Get Ready

A Look at the people and read the words. Write the number of the words in the correct place in the picture (1–10). Use each word once.

1.	tall
2.	glasses
3.	young
4.	middle-aged
5.	blond hair
6.	short hair
7.	curly hair
8.	large earrings
9.	short
10.	mustache

B Read the sentences.
Write *T* for true, or *F* for false.

1. ____ Sandra has short hair.
2. ____ George has a mustache.
3. ____ Kathi has earrings.

4. ____ Amy is short.
5. ____ Tony has curly hair.
6. ____ Erik is tall.

 Start Talking 🎞

A Look at the conversation and listen.

Erik: Do you know Amy?
Sandra: I don't know. What does she look like?
Erik: She's kind of short, and she has curly hair.
Sandra: Oh, yes. I know her.

Pair work **B** Practice the conversation.
Then practice again, using the information about the people in Get Ready.
Can you think of any other words to describe people?

3 Listen In

(A) **Look at the people below. Which words in Get Ready could you use to describe them?**

(B) **Who are they talking about? Listen and draw a line from the name to the correct person.**

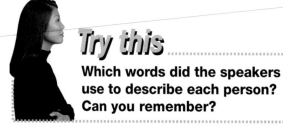

◄ **Brian Morgan**

◄ **Nina Hansen**

◄ **Michael Shea**

◄ **Annie Jones**

(C) **Do the speakers *know* these people? Listen again and check (✔) the names of the people they know.**

Try this
Which words did the speakers use to describe each person? Can you remember?

4 Say It Right

(A) **Some sounds are not pronounced clearly in rapid speech. Listen and pay attention to the underlined letters.**

1. *What does she look like?*

2. *I don't know.*

3. *Is she tall?*

4. *Does he have glasses?*

5. *Yes, he does.*

(B) **Listen again and practice.**

Try this
Make up two more examples of your own.
Then practice with a partner.

5 Focus In

A Look at the chart. When do we use *does/doesn't*? When do we use *do/don't*?

Questions and answers with *do/does*	
Do you know George?	Yes, I **do**.
Do they know your boss?	No, they **don't**.
Does he have glasses?	Yes, he **does**.
Does she wear earrings?	No, she **doesn't**.
Does he have curly hair?	No, he **doesn't**. He has straight hair.

B Match the questions and answers. Then practice them with a partner.

1. Do you know Lisa?   a. No, you don't.
2. Does she have long hair?   b. Yes, they do.
3. Do they wear glasses?   c. No, he doesn't.
4. Does he have curly hair?   d. Yes, I do.
5. Do I know him?   e. No, she doesn't.

C Fill in the missing information. Then ask your partner the questions.

1. _____ your parents wear glasses?   4. _____ your best friend have curly hair?
2. _____ you know my English teacher?   5. _____ your best friend speak English?
3. _____ you know my best friend?   6. _____ your sisters wear earrings?

6 Talk Some More

A Write the words in the correct places.

(*isn't*) (*know*) (*do*) (*does*)
(*has*) (*is*) (*look*) (*have*)

Simon: _____ you know my friend Paul?
Wendy: I'm not sure. What does he _____ like?
Simon: He _____ blond, curly hair.
Wendy: _____ he tall?
Simon: No, he _____. He's kind of average height.
Wendy: Does he _____ glasses?
Simon: Yes, he _____.
Wendy: Oh, yeah. I _____ him.

B Check your answers.

Pair work **C** Practice the conversation with a partner.
Use your own information.

Spotlight
yeah = yes
in casual speech

Work In Pairs — Student A

Student B: Use page 28

(A) Look at the people.
Then read the statements to your partner. Your partner will answer 'True' or 'False.'

1. All three women have earrings.

2. Two of the men have dark hair.

3. One of the women has short hair.

(B) Ask your partner questions.
Fill in the missing information.

What does Sally look like?

		IS	HAS
Dave	☐	tall	short, black hair/glasses
Sally	☐		
Richard	☐	average height	short, brown hair
Patricia	☐		
Bruce	☐	average height	blond hair/glasses
Jean	☐		

(C) Look at the picture again. Write the number of the person next to the correct name.

Try this

Make up three sentences describing famous people.

Example: Tom Cruise is short and has dark brown hair.

1 _____

_____

2 _____

_____

3 _____

_____

▶ Share your sentences with your partner. Were any similar?

Work In Pairs   Student B

A Look at the people.
Then read the statements to your partner. Your partner will answer 'True' or 'False.'

1. *All three men have glasses.*

2. *Two of the women have curly hair.*

3. *One of the men has blond hair.*

B Ask your partner questions.
Fill in the missing information.

What does Dave look like?

		IS	HAS
Dave	☐		
Sally	☐	average height	long, curly hair/earrings
Richard	☐		
Patricia	☐	short	long, black hair
Bruce	☐		
Jean	☐	average height	short, black hair

C Look at the picture again. Write the number of the person next to the correct name.

Try this

Make up three sentences describing famous people.

Example: Tom Cruise is short and has dark brown hair.

1 _____

_____

2 _____

_____

3 _____

_____

▶ **Share your sentences with your partner. Were any similar?**

Express Yourself

A Think of a person in your class. Don't tell anyone!

Group work **B** Your classmates will ask questions and guess the person. Answer the questions only if they begin with *is* or *does*.

Is he tall?

Yes, he is.

?

?

?

Think About It

In many cultures, it's OK to ask people certain questions but not others. In most cultures, people are interested in other people's age. In most English-speaking cultures, it's generally rude to ask a person's age. In your culture:

• *is it OK to ask adults their age?*
• *does it make a difference whether they're men or women?*
• *is it OK to ask children about their age?*

Write About It

A Read the following part of a letter to a pen pal.

B Write your own description to a pen pal on a piece of paper. Don't write your name!

C Mix up the papers and take one. Read the description and find the person.

Dear Shawn,

Thank you for your message. I'm glad you are my pen pal. You want to know what I look like? Well, I'm tall, I have long hair, and I wear glasses. Oh, and I often wear big earrings. I'll send you some photos.

Read On   Finding the Right Look

• *Strategy: Inferring vocabulary*

Is personal appearance really important? Some companies want you to think so.

An 'image consulting company' can help you change your look. Just send them a photo of yourself, answer some questions about your job or your hobbies—and, of course, send money! They will send your picture back to you, together with ideas for new clothes, hairstyles, glasses, and jewelry that are right for you. They say they can help you plan a new look for work, for play, or even to find the perfect mate. They will even tell you where to shop!

The image consultants give women tips about makeup, and give men advice about their mustache or beard, if they have one. They teach you the best way to introduce yourself to other people. They also offer tips on what to say in job interviews, and how to act when eating out. By helping people change their style, they believe those people will feel better about themselves.

Look at the article again, and find words or phrases with the same meaning.
The first one has been done for you.

1. The way you look   *personal appearance* _____

2. Things you do in your free time _____

3. The ideal husband or wife _____

4. Hints _____

5. Eating in a restaurant _____

Talk About It

⭕ Are there image consulting companies in your country?

⭕ Do you think these companies are a good idea? Why or why not?

Review

1 Vocabulary Review

A Fill in the chart with words you learned in this unit.

Hair	Height	Age

B What other words are used to describe people's appearance? Note any others you remember.

Do you know Steve?

Well, he has sunglasses...

Hmm...What does he look like?

2 Grammar Review

A Fill in the blanks.

1. _____ you know Amy?   Yes, I _____.
2. _____ they know your boss?   No, they _____.
3. _____ he have glasses?   Yes, he _____.
4. _____ she wear earrings?   No, she _____.
5. _____ he have curly hair?   No, he _____. He has straight hair.

B Write questions or statements using the words below.

1. (know) _____
2. (hair) _____
3. (earrings) _____
4. (tall) _____

3 Log On

Practice more with the language and topics you studied on the *Expressions* website:

http://expressions.heinle.com

Goals

○ *Asking and answering questions about where people are from*

Where are you from?

1 Get Ready

A Look at the people.
Where are they from?
Write the number of the country
next to the correct people (1–6).

1. Brazil
2. Japan
3. Mexico
4. Taiwan
5. Canada
6. Korea

B Circle the cities. Underline the countries.
Which ones go together? Write them on a piece of paper.

Egypt Turkey Peru Istanbul Sydney Ireland

Lima Paris Cairo Australia France Dublin

2 Start Talking

A Look at the conversation and listen.

Stan: Where are you from?
Maria: Mexico. How about you?
Stan: Canada. Are you on vacation?
Maria: Yes, I am.

Pair work **B** Practice the conversation with a partner.
Then practice again, using different country names.

3 Listen In

(A) Listen and circle the names you hear. Then write them in the chart.

Anita	Paul	Tomoko	Winston
Steve	John	Anne	Patricia

(B) Where are they from? What are they doing? Listen again and fill in the chart.

Name	From?	On vacation?
_____	_____	_____
_____	_____	_____
_____	_____	_____

Try this
**What does the first woman
say to show interest?
Can you remember?**

Where are you from?

4 Say It Right

(A) Which countries have the same stress pattern? Number them (1–5).

1. Mex • i • co
2. Bra • zil
3. Ko • re • a
4. Eng • land
5. In • do • ne • sia

_____ Ma • lay • sia
_____ Ven • e • zue • la
___1___ Can • a • da
_____ Tai • wan
_____ Swe • den

(B) Listen and check your answers.

(C) Listen again and practice.

Try this
**Pronounce the names of the
countries in Get Ready. Pay
attention to the stress patterns.**

5 Focus In

A Look at the chart.

Is/Are and Do/Does

Where **are** you from?	**I'm** from Turkey.
Where **is** Amy from?	She**'s** from Canada.
Where **does** Jake come from?	He **comes** from Australia.
Where **do** Alec and Suzie live?	They **live** in San Francisco.

B Fill in the missing information.

1. Where _____ Sally from?
2. Where _____ Ric and Luc from?
3. Where _____ Hyo Soon live?
4. Where _____ you come from?
5. Where _____ Jake come from?
6. Where _____ Tomo and Saeko live?

C Draw lines to match the questions and answers.
Then practice with a partner using your own information.

1. What's your name?
2. Where are you from?
3. What do you do?
4. Are you on vacation?
5. Are you married?

   a. I'm a doctor.
   b. Yes, I am.
   c. Yes, this is my husband.
   d. Maria.
   e. I'm from New York.

6 Talk Some More

Spotlight
What do you do?
and *What are you doing?*
have very different meanings.

A Write the letter of the correct response
in each blank to make a conversation.

Kelly: What's your name?
Maria: _____
Kelly: Where are you from?
Maria: _____
Kelly: Are you on vacation?
Maria: _____
Kelly: What do you do?
Maria: _____

   a. I'm a student.
   b. Yes, I am.
   c. Maria.
   d. I'm from Mexico.

B Check your answers.

Pair work

C Practice the conversation with a partner. Use your own information.

Work In Pairs (Student A)

A Look at the women in the picture. Where do you think they are?

B Look at the information. Then fill in the chart with as much information as you can about the three women's names, where they are from, and what they're doing.

- *Mary is from Australia.*
- *Ms. Lee isn't from Australia or Brazil.*
- *Gina isn't from Taiwan or Australia.*
- *Ms. Oliveira is from Brazil.*

Name	From?	Doing what?

C Read your information to your partner. Listen to your partner's information. Finish the chart. Ask your partner questions to check your answers.

Try this

Write sentences about the three women.

1. _____

2. _____

3. _____

Where are you from?   **35**

Work In Pairs Student B

A Look at the women in the picture. Where do you think they are?

B Look at the information. Then fill in the chart with as much information as you can about the three women's names, where they are from, and what they're doing.

- *Ms. Stewart isn't from Taiwan or Brazil.*
- *Jenny is from Taiwan.*
- *Mary is on vacation.*
- *Two of the people are students.*

Name	From?	Doing what?

C Read your information to your partner. Listen to your partner's information. Finish the chart. Ask your partner questions to check your answers.

Try this

Write sentences about the three women.

1 _____

2 _____

3 _____

Express Yourself

 A Think of the name of a person from another country. It can be someone you know, someone you met before, or someone famous.

 B Work in groups. Take turns asking questions about each person. Ask as many questions as you can.

Where is he from?

What does he do?

Why is he famous?

Think About It

When you meet a person for the first time, some questions are OK to ask and others may not be. Which questions do you think are OK?

- *Where are you from?*
- *How old are you?*

- *Do you have any children?*
- *How much money do you make?*

- *What's your name?*
- *What do you do?*

Does everyone in your class agree? What other questions are OK to ask in your culture? What questions are not OK?

Write About It

 A Look at the hotel registration form.

HOTEL RICHMOND PLAZA

Guest Registration

Please fill in the following information.

Family Name ___Gallagher___

First Names ___Jeremy Spencer___

Nationality ___Australian___

Passport Number ___A3266790___

Date of Birth (M/D/Y) ___7/31/55___

Length of Stay ___4___ nights

Home Address ___31, Melville Street,___
___Concord West, NSW 25491,___
___Australia___

Thank You

HOTEL RICHMOND PLAZA

Guest Registration

Please fill in the following information.

Family Name _____

First Names _____

Nationality _____

Passport Number _____

Date of Birth (M/D/Y) _____

Length of Stay _____ nights

Home Address _____

_____

_____

Thank You

 B Now fill in the form. Use your own information.

I'm from Portland...but which one?

• Strategy: Inferring content

Portland is a popular name for cities in English-speaking countries. Which Portland is each person describing?

#1 My Portland is next to the Atlantic Ocean. It's a beautiful town. We have many homes from the 19th century. On weekends we like to hike or bike on trails by the waterfront or in nearby forests. Our most famous food is lobster. Our city was founded in 1786. Its name came from Portland, England. We love living here. You should come to visit us.

#2 My Portland is at a place where two rivers meet. Its nickname is the 'Bridge City' because we have eight bridges. On weekends we enjoy biking, jogging, or sailing. Nearby are mountains where we can ski in the winter. We are proud of our local salmon and wine. Our city was founded in 1845 and its name came from Portland, Maine. It's a great place to live, and we love visitors.

#3 My Portland is on a small island near the Atlantic Ocean. People have lived here for thousands of years. Our island is very green, and our beaches are sandy. Many people enjoy diving, windsurfing, sailing, and rock climbing here. Tourists like to visit our castles and churches and to drink tea in our tearooms. Portland is a very special place. Come see us!

Portland, Oregon

Portland, Maine

Portland, England

Write the number of the paragraph next to the correct place.

Portland, Oregon: Paragraph _____
Portland, England: Paragraph _____
Portland, Maine: Paragraph _____

Now circle the vocabulary in the text that helped you decide.

Talk About It

○ Which of these cities would you most like to visit? What would you like to do there?

○ Have you ever visited a very interesting city?

○ Which place have you always wanted to visit? Why?

12 Review

1 Vocabulary Review

A Fill in the names of the countries you learned in this unit.

Asia	The Americas	Others
_____	_____	_____
_____	_____	_____
_____	_____	_____
_____	_____	_____

B Which of these countries would you like to visit? Why?

2 Grammar Review

A Fill in the blanks.

1. Where _____ you from?   _____ from Mexico.
2. Where _____ Laura from?   _____ from Scotland.
3. Where _____ Steve from?   _____ from Taiwan.
4. What ____ you _____?   _____ a teacher.
5. What _____ Laura _____?   _____ a student.
6. What _____ John _____?   _____ on vacation.

B Circle the best response in each pair.

1. What do you do?   **a.** I'm from Paris.   **b.** I'm a student here.
2. Do you come from India?   **a.** Yes, I do.   **b.** Yes, I am.
3. Where are you from?   **a.** I am in California.   **b.** I come from California.
4. Is she a student?   **a.** No, she works here.   **b.** No, she doesn't.

3 Log On

Practice more with the language and topics you studied on the *Expressions* website:

http://expressions.heinle.com

Make yourself at home.

1 Get Ready

A Look at the words.
Are they names of food or drink?

1.	juice
2.	cookies
3.	tea
4.	coffee
5.	bread
6.	orange
7.	cola
8.	apple
9.	milk
10.	sandwich

B Write the missing information in the correct place in the pictures.

- *Thanks. I like it a lot, too.*
- *Yes, please.*
- *Thanks.*

Welcome. Come in and make yourself at home.

Your new apartment is really nice.

Would you like some tea?

2 Start Talking

A Look at the conversation in Get Ready and listen.

Pair work **B** Practice the conversation with a partner. Offer other food and drink items. Try using the following expressions:

- *Hi. Come in and have a seat.*
- *I really like your new place.*
- *Would you like something to drink?*

3 Listen In

A Look at the pictures below. Which rooms can you see in the man's home?

B Listen and check (✔) the words you hear.

_____ tea	_____ juice	_____ cookies	_____ bedroom	_____ kitchen
_____ coffee	_____ water	_____ cakes	_____ living room	_____ bathroom

C Listen again and write the number of the conversation above the correct picture (1–3).

Try this

What word does the second man use to show surprise? Can you remember?

4 Say It Right

A Sometimes the letter *c* sounds like /s/ and sometimes like /k/.
Circle the ones that sound like /s/. Underline the ones that sound like /k/.

1. A: Come in. Make yourself comfortable.
   B: Wow. This place is really nice.

2. A: Would you like some juice or coffee?
   B: Thanks. A cup of coffee sounds great.

3. A: How about some cookies?
   B: No, thanks. But can I have some water, please?
   A: Of course.

Try this

Make up two more examples of your own. Exchange your sentences with your partner. Circle the /s/ sounds; underline the /k/ sounds.

B Listen and check your answers.

C Listen again and practice.

5 Focus In

A) Look at the chart.

Would/may	
Would you like some coffee?	Yes, please.
Would you like some tea?	No, thanks. But **may** I have some water?
May I use your bathroom?	Of course. It's the second door on the right.
May I have some juice?	**Would** you like orange or apple?

B) Change these sentences into polite offers.

1. Come in! _____Would you like to come in?_____
2. Have some juice! _____
3. I want some water! _____May I have some water?_____
4. I want to use the bathroom! _____
5. I want some more! _____

C) Where would you hear these sentences? Write the number next to the correct place. (There may be more than one answer for some.)

1. May I help you?   _____ At a restaurant.
2. Take a look around.   _____ At a friend's house.
3. Please turn off your cell phone. _____ At a store.
4. Would you like to order?   _____ At a movie theater.

6 Talk Some More

A) Number the sentences to make a conversation (1–6).

Eric: _____ Thanks a lot.
Phoebe: _____ Sure. Here you are.
Eric: _____ May I have some coffee, please?
Eric: _____ Thanks. Nice place.
Phoebe: _____ Hi. Come in.
Phoebe: _____ Thanks. Would you like some tea or coffee?

Spotlight
Thanks a lot is stronger than Thanks.

B) Check your answers.

Pair work

C) Practice the conversation. Then practice again offering different items.

Work In Pairs Student A

A Look at the pictures below. What types of food or drink can you see? Check with your partner.

B Look at the pictures. Write what you think the host is saying in the speech bubbles.

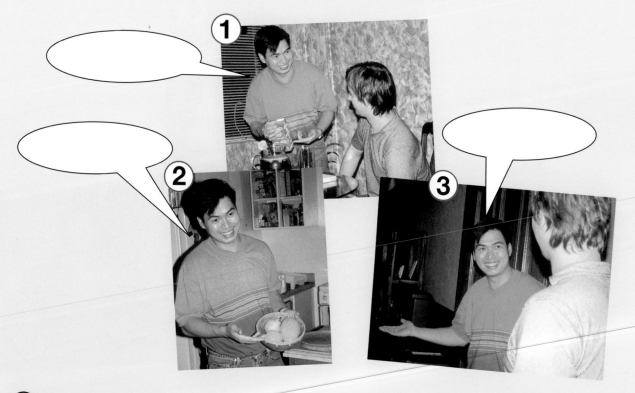

C Read the information to your partner. Ask your partner to tell you which picture (4–6) matches yours (1–3). Then write the conversation.

```
Host: _____
Guest: _____
Host: _____
Guest: _____
Host: _____
Guest: _____
```

Try this

Try the conversation again using the different foods and drinks from Get Ready.

Work In Pairs Student B

A Look at the pictures below. What types of food or drink can you see? Check with your partner.

B Look at the pictures. Write what you think the guest is saying in the speech bubbles.

C Read the information to your partner. Ask your partner to tell you which picture (1–3) matches yours (4–6). Then write the conversation.

Host:_____

Guest: _____

Host: _____

Guest: _____

Host: _____

Guest: _____

Try this

Try the conversation again using the different foods and drinks from Get Ready.

8 Express Yourself

A How many food and drink items can you remember from Get Ready?
Write at least four in the space.

○
○
○
○
○
○

B Offer your classmates the items on your list.
Write their first names next to the items they accept.
Write a different name for each item.

9 Think About It

When you visit someone's home for the first time, do you like to look around? If so, you're not unusual. Most people love to see how others live.

• How about in your culture? Is it OK to ask your host to show you around? Why/why not?

10 Write About It

A Look at the housewarming invitation and the reply.

WE'VE MOVED!

Please come to our housewarming, and help us celebrate in our new apartment. 8:00 p.m. on May 30.

Benny and Paula
44 Wright Avenue
Apt. 3A
Southside Park
Tel: 555-2981
Email: bennyandpaula@email.net

Get Msg New Msg R

Subject: Thanks for the invitation...
From: sharon@homemail.com
To: bennyandpaula@email.net

Hi Benny and Paula

Thanks for the invitation. I'd love to come to your housewarming. I'll see you next Friday night.

Take care,
Sharon

Toggle Attachment Pane

B Make up your own housewarming invitation. Pass it to several students. Write replies to the ones you receive.

11 Read On — Good Guests and Good Hosts

• *Strategy: Scanning*

How would you make your guests feel at home?

Angela Ascanio, Venezuela

Venezuelans usually invite only close friends or relatives to our homes. At home, we always offer guests a cup of strong, black coffee. Visitors usually bring a gift, like flowers. At meals we sit on chairs around a table. We eat with knives and forks, though many people just use the fork. After guests finish eating, they put the knife and fork in the center of their plate.

Jariya Anukulsupart, Thailand

We don't tell our dinner guests what time to arrive. In the city we sit on chairs around a table, but in the countryside we sit on mats on the floor. We hold our spoon in our right hand and our fork in our left. We push food onto the spoon with the fork. We drink water or beer with our meal. When we finish, we put our fork and spoon together on the plate.

Mohammed Al-Swailem, Saudi Arabia

In Saudi Arabia we have a special room for visitors. We usually sit on cushions on the floor. When a guest visits, we serve strong coffee or sweet mint tea. We never serve alcohol. When guests finish drinking, they cover the cup with their hand. When they finish eating, the host must offer more food, but the guests should politely say no. My father generally invites only men to visit him. My mother invites only women. A man must not bring a gift for the wife of the house, but he may bring gifts for the children.

Complete the chart with information from the article.
If there is no information, put *X* in the box.

	Venezuela	Thailand	Saudi Arabia
What gift to bring...			
What to drink...			
Where to sit at dinner...			
What to do after eating or drinking...			

---

*T*alk About It

○ In your culture, do you often invite people to your home?

○ When you visit someone, do you take a gift? What would you take?

○ In your culture, what should a good host do?

1 Vocabulary Review

A Fill in the chart with words you learned in this unit.

Hot drinks
_____
_____
_____
_____

Cold drinks
_____
_____
_____
_____

Food
_____
_____
_____
_____
_____

B Which do you usually offer guests? Which don't you offer?

2 Grammar Review

A Fill in the blanks.

1. _____ / _____ at home.
2. _____ _____ use your bathroom?
3. _____ _____ like some tea?
4. No, thanks. But _____ _____ have some water, please?
5. Is it OK if _____ _____ around?

B Write the correct sentences on the right.

1. your/may/use/I/telephone _____ *May I use your telephone?*
2. I/just/water/have/may/please _____
3. like/sandwich/you/would/a _____
4. apartment/wow!/this/nice/a/is _____
5. coffee/a/sounds/cup/great/of _____

3 Log On

Practice more with the language and topics you studied on the *Expressions* website:

http://expressions.heinle.com

Make yourself at home.

How much is this sweater?

Get Ready

A Look at the advertisement. Write the number of the item next to the correct picture.

1. T-shirts
2. sweaters
3. shorts
4. jeans
5. shirts
6. shoes
7. dresses

SALE! SALE! SALE! SALE

$16
$7.99
$3.50
$8.60
$19.50
$29.99
$14

One Day Only!

B Look at the words. Are they used to describe colors or patterns? Which words can be used to describe the items in the ad?

1. blue   3. striped   5. brown   7. purple   9. checked
2. floral   4. green   6. yellow   8. red   10. white

Start Talking

A Look at the conversation and listen.

Eugene: I need a sweater.
Jill: Here are some sweaters
Eugene: How much are they?
Jill: $16.

Pair work **B** Practice the conversation with a partner.
Then practice again, using different items from the ad.

3 Listen In

(A) Look at the items in the picture below. What colors are they?

(B) Listen and circle the words you hear.

1. How much are the shoes/sweaters?
2. How much are they/is it?
3. How many do you need/want?

4. What are you looking for/at?
5. How much is the black/red dress?
6. Do you take personal/traveler's checks?

(C) Listen again and write the name of each item next to the correct price.

$22.99 _____ $14.00 _____
$2.99 _____ $40.00 _____
$15.00 _____ $16.00 _____
$4.50 _____ $60.00 _____

Try this...

What word does the woman use to show she likes the dress? Can you remember?

4 Say It Right

(A) When we want to check if we heard something correctly, we can use rising (⤴) intonation.

(B) Listen and mark the intonation in the three conversations.

(C) Listen again and practice.

5 Focus In

A Look at the chart.

How much/How many	
How much is the sweater?	It's $36.
How much are the shoes?	They're $48 a pair.
How many T-shirts are on the table?	One.
How many shorts do you need?	I need two pairs.

B Fill in the blanks with *how much/how many*.

1. _____ pairs of jeans do you want?
2. _____ is a new pair of shoes?
3. _____ are his pants?
4. _____ shirts does she have?
5. _____ does his sweater cost?

C Number the lines in order to make a conversation. Then practice with a partner.

_____ A: They're on sale. Five dollars each.

_____ A: How many do you want?

_____ A: May I help you?

_____ B: Yes, please. How much are the T-shirts?

_____ B: Um, I'll take four.

_____ B: Five dollars? Great. I want some blue ones.

6 Talk Some More

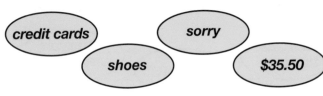

A Write the words in the correct spaces.

credit cards

sorry

shoes

$35.50

Customer: I'll take the sweater and the _____.

Clerk: That'll be _____, please.

Customer: Do you take _____?

Clerk: No, we don't. _____. Cash only.

Spotlight

When a price has dollars AND cents, people often say the numbers only. $35.50 can be said as:
Thirty-five dollars and fifty cents or *Thirty-five fifty.*

B Check your answers.

Pair work

C Practice the conversation. Then practice again with different items and prices.

A Look at the pictures. Write descriptions of the items, following the example. Read your list to your partner to compare.

> *Example* _a red and yellow checked shirt_
> - _____
> - _____
> - _____
>
> - _____
> - _____
> - _____

SALE

$10.95

$15.99

$4.99

$17.25

B Ask your partner for the missing prices. Write them on the price tags. Listen to your partner's questions and answer them.

C Imagine you are a clerk. Make up a shopping conversation with your partner. Take turns writing each line. Then practice the conversation.

> Clerk: _____
> Customer: _____
> Clerk: _____
> Customer: _____
> Clerk: _____
> Customer: _____
> Clerk: _____
> Customer: _____

Work In Pairs — Student B

A Look at the pictures. Write descriptions of the items, following the example. Read your list to your partner to compare.

Example a red and yellow checked shirt

- _____
- _____
- _____

- _____
- _____
- _____

$10.95

SALE

$18.50

$14.50

$8.60

B Ask your partner for the missing prices. Write them on the price tags. Listen to your partner's questions and answer them.

C Imagine you are a customer. Make up a shopping conversation with your partner. Take turns writing each line. Then practice the conversation.

Clerk: _____

Customer: _____

Clerk: _____

Customer: _____

Clerk: _____

Customer: _____

Clerk: _____

Customer: _____

8 Express Yourself

A Look at the items. How much do they usually cost where you live?
Write the prices in the 'My Price' list. (Use your own currency.)

	My Price	No. 1	No. 2	No. 3
jeans				
shirts				
shoes				
sweaters				
T-shirts				

B Ask three partners for their prices and fill in the lists.
Then choose the items you want to buy and practice paying.

9 *Think About It*

In some cultures, sales clerks closely follow customers who are shopping for clothes or other items. Some customers like this, but some don't.

• How about in your culture? How do customers feel about close attention from sales clerks?

10 Write About It

A Look at the advertisements.

For Sale
Whitewater washing machine.
Almost new. $550
Call Rick at 3954-7945

Best price! $350
Dining table and chairs
for immediate sale.
Al Lamond Tel: 555-0286

...or Sale
2 tickets to Cassandra Wilson concert
$35 each–or make me an offer.
Call Mary at 555-5497

Must Sell $275
King size water bed.
Only six months old.
Owner going overseas.
Contact Paul Rice
Fax: 555-3956

B Make an advertisement to sell something of your own. Write it on a piece of paper.

How much is this sweater?

11 Read On   Retro Fashion

• Strategy: Looking for main ideas

Good fashion never dies.

Many years after they went away, the 1970s came back into fashion. After more than twenty years, young people started to wear the clothes that their parents, aunts, and uncles loved at their age. In the United States, second-hand stores, called 'resale shops' or 'thrift shops,' sell the popular items of that era.

At these shops, men can buy bell-bottom jeans, polyester suits, wide neckties, and plaid pants. In addition to bell-bottom jeans, women can find mini-dresses, vinyl mini-skirts, and go-go boots with high platform soles. This look became so popular again that some companies designed new clothes copying the style of this era.

How much do these retro fashions cost at a resale shop? It's not too hard to find a mini-dress for as low as $12, $5–10 for a jacket, $5 for a skirt or a pair of long pants, and you might get a T-shirt, belt, or a tie for only $1! The new copies of these styles cost a lot more.

Check (✔) the main idea for each paragraph in each pair.

Paragraph 1

_____ Fashions of the 1970s are now sold only in second-hand stores.

_____ The styles of the 1970s became popular again many years later.

Paragraph 2

_____ There are many types of '70s items for sale for both men and women.

_____ Both men and women can wear bell-bottom jeans.

Paragraph 3

_____ The original items from the 1970s are sold for low prices.

_____ New clothes cost more than clothes from the 1970s.

Talk About It

○ What do young people in your country think about wearing second-hand clothing?

○ Which styles are popular with young people in your country?

○ Do you like to follow fashion trends? Why or why not?

12 Review

1 Vocabulary Review

(A) Fill in the chart with words you learned in this unit.

Men's Clothes	Women's Clothes	Both

(B) Which of these items do you usually wear? Which do you never wear?

2 Grammar Review

How much are the T-shirts?

(A) Fill in the blanks.

1. How much _____ the T-shirts?
2. _____ $4.50.
3. How many _____ you need?
4. How much _____ the red dress?
5. _____ you take personal checks?

(B) Make up questions about shopping with the words shown.

1. (shoes) _____
2. (want) _____
3. (how many) _____
4. (credit cards) _____
5. (look for) _____

3 Log On

Practice more with the language and topics you studied on the *Expressions* website:

http://expressions.heinle.com

Goals

○ *Asking for and identifying locations in buildings* ○ *Giving directions*

Is there a pool?

1 Get Ready

A Write the number of the location in the correct place in the hotel.

1. pool
2. front desk
3. business center
4. newsstand
5. restaurant
6. laundry
7. health club
8. coffee shop

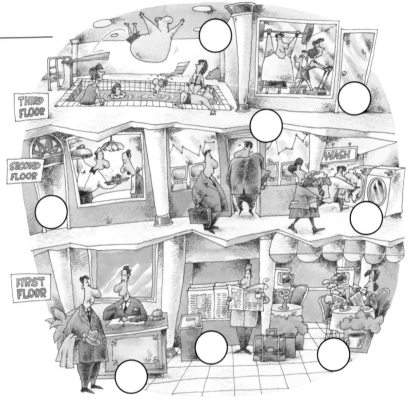

B Read the sentences.
Write *T* for true, or *F* for false.

1. _____ The coffee shop is on the first floor.
2. _____ The pool is on the second floor.
3. _____ The health club is on the third floor.

4. _____ The business center is next to the pool.
5. _____ The pool is to the left of the health club.
6. _____ The newsstand is between the front desk and the coffee shop.

2 Start Talking

A Look at the conversation and listen.

Guest: Excuse me.
Clerk: Yes, sir?
Guest: Is there a business center in this hotel?
Clerk: Yes, there is. It's on the second floor, next to the restaurant.

Pair work

B Practice the conversation with a partner.
Then practice again, using different hotel facilities.

3 Listen In

A Look at the pictures below. Write the facility where you can find each one.

B Listen and write the number of the conversation (1–4) next to the facilities pictured below.

_____   _____   _____

_____   _____   _____

C Listen again and write the number of the conversation next to the directions.

_____ Take the elevator to the second floor. Turn left, and you'll find it next to the business center.
_____ Just go down those stairs right there and turn right.
_____ Take the elevator to the third floor and turn left.
_____ Go up the stairs and turn right.

Try this ....
Can you tell me how to get there?
You heard three questions with the same meaning. What are they? Can you remember?

4 Say It Right

A Important information in a sentence is sometimes stressed. Listen to the examples. What is more important—the facility or where it is?

B Listen and check (✔) the correct column in the chart.

C Listen again and check your answers.

	Facility	Where
Example 1	✔	
Example 2		✔
1.		
2.		
3.		
4.		
5.		
6.		

5 Focus In

A Look at the chart.

Prepositions: *on/next to/between*	
Is there a business center in this hotel?	Yes, there is. It's **on** the first/second/third floor. It's **next to** the fitness center. It's **between** the restaurant and the laundry.

B Fill in the blanks. Use *between*, *next to*, or *on*.

1. A: Is there a pool?
   B: Yes, there is. It's _____ the third floor, _____ the fitness center.

2. A: I'm looking for the business center.
   B: Oh, it's _____ the second floor _____ the restaurant and the laundry.

3. A: Are there any places to eat?
   B: Yes, there are. There's a coffee shop _____ the first floor _____ the newsstand.
   And there's a restaurant _____ the second floor _____ the business center.

C Look at the hotel in Get Ready. Answer the questions.

1. Excuse me. Is there a business center in this hotel?_____
2. Excuse me. Is there a laundry in this hotel?   _____
3. Excuse me. Is there a newsstand in this hotel?   _____
4. Excuse me. Is there a health club in this hotel?   _____

6 Talk Some More

A Look at the hotel in Get Ready. Fill in the missing information.

Guest: _____
Clerk: Yes, ma'am?
Guest: _____ health club in this hotel?
Clerk: Yes, _____.
Guest: How do I get there?
Clerk: Take the elevator to the third floor.
       It's _____.

Spotlight

Ma'am is the polite way to address a woman. The polite way to address a man is *Sir*.

B Check your answers.

Pair work

C Practice the conversation with a partner.
Then practice again using different facilities in Get Ready.

Work In Pairs (Student A)

A Look at the hotel in the picture. Ask if your partner's hotel has the same facilities as yours. List the facilities in your partner's hotel.

B Where are the facilities in your partner's hotel? Are they the same as yours? Ask your partner. How many differences can you find? Mark the location of your partner's facilities on your picture.

Try this

Write sentences about the facilities in your building.
Then compare them with your partner's.

Work In Pairs   Student B

A Look at the hotel in the picture. Ask if your partner's hotel has the same facilities as yours. List the facilities in your partner's hotel.

B Where are the facilities in your partner's hotel?
Are they the same as yours? Ask your partner. How many differences can you find?
Mark the location of your partner's facilities on your picture.

Try this

Write sentences about the facilities in your building.
Then compare them with your partner's.

8 Express Yourself

(A) What facilities would you like in a hotel? Check (✔) the right answer for you. Would you like a...

_____ health club? _____ business center?

_____ restaurant? _____ pool?

_____ coffee shop? _____ laundry?

 Pair work

(B) Ask a partner and circle your partner's answers.

9 Think About It

Many cultures use street names and numbers in their addresses. Some cultures don't. For example, in a huge city like Tokyo, where there are few street names and numbers, people are very good at giving directions.

Well, you take the subway to Shinjuku Station. Take exit 28C, turn right and walk for three blocks. You will see a police box. Turn left and walk two more blocks. On your left, you will see a large blue building. Make another left and walk one more block. Right in front of you will be a small coffee shop called Coffee Time. I'll meet you there.

- What about in your culture? Are there numbered street addresses in your country? Are there street names? How do you usually give directions?

10 Write About It

(A) Look at the note.

Dear Bill,

We're meeting in the business center.
Take the elevator to the third floor.
Turn right and go to the end of the hall.
The business center is on the left.

(B) A new student is joining your class. Write a note explaining how to get from the front door of the building to your classroom.

Read On · A World of Services

• **Strategy:** Scanning

The phone book is a great way to find goods and services nearby.

Pet Hotel
- Dog & cat boarding
- Loving care
- House boarding available
- Cat roomettes
- Music and special lighting
- All breed dog grooming

- Pick up and delivery service
- Reservations requested
- Labrador Retriever puppies for sale

We never close!
68 Oakridge Road, 555-4546

Wordsmith's
BOOK COMPANY & CAFE

New and used books

Over 100,000 titles

Readings by authors

Good coffee and tea

Tasty foods, tempting desserts

No one will hurry you

Open every day 10 a.m. – 10 p.m.
Courthouse Square, 555-2125

SUDZ'S LAUNDROMAT

Drop off or self service

Clean and modern

Helpful attendants

Tan or watch big screen TV

Espresso / Beer / Mini Deli

Open 7 days a week
7 a.m. – 11 p.m.
3107 Monroe, 555-7896

CAMPING WORLD RV-PARK
- *Pull-thrus & full hook-ups*
- *Tent sites*
- *Clean restrooms & showers*
- *Cable TV, phone*
- *Laundry*

- *Groceries*
- *Game rooms*
- *Exercise room*
- *Fishing*
- *Swimming pool*

Open May through September
8 miles east on Highway 231, 555-3849

Where can you...? Check (✔) the boxes.

	Laundromat	Bookstore	RV-Park	Pet Hotel
Eat and drink				
Watch TV				
Buy a dog				
Get a tan				

Which place is...? Check (✔) the boxes.

	Laundromat	Bookstore	RV-Park	Pet Hotel
Always open				
Outside of town				
Open 5 months a year				
Open 16 hours a day				

Talk About It

- What surprises you about each business?
- Which business do you think will make a lot of money? Why?
- Which of the businesses do you have in your country? Do they make a lot of money?

1 Vocabulary Review

A Write the names of four facilities you learned in this unit. Then write where they are in the hotel in Get Ready.

Facility	Where?

B In which other places could you also find these facilities?

2 Grammar Review

A Fill in the blanks.

1. The pool is _____ the second floor.
2. The laundry is next _____ the pool.
3. The business center is _____ the restaurant and the newsstand.
4. Take the elevator _____ the third floor.
5. Go _____ the stairs and turn right.

B Check (✔) the correct sentence in each pair.

1. _____ The coffee shop is on the third floor.
   _____ The coffee shop is on third floor.
2. _____ Is the laundry on the four floor?
   _____ Is the laundry on the fourth floor?
3. _____ The pool is next the health club.
   _____ The pool is next to the health club.
4. _____ Take the elevator to the first floor and turn to right.
   _____ Take the elevator to the first floor and turn right.

Where is the pool?

It's on the second floor

3 Log On

Practice more with the language and topics you studied on the *Expressions* website:

http://expressions.heinle.com

Goals

○ Describing procedures   ○ Narrating a sequence

First, you turn it on.

1 Get Ready

A Look at the words.
Write the number next
to the correct item (1–6).

1. fax machine
2. cassette player
3. CD player
4. answering machine
5. computer
6. VCR

B Answer the questions. Then compare your answers with a partner's.

1. Which machines use a tape? _____

2. Which machines use a disk? _____

3. Which of these machines do you use often? _____

4. Which have you never used? _____

2 Start Talking

A Look at the conversation and listen.

Belinda: Do you know how to use a computer?

Kate: No, it looks difficult.

Belinda: It's easy. First, you turn it on. Next, put in
a disk. Then, you open a file. That's all.

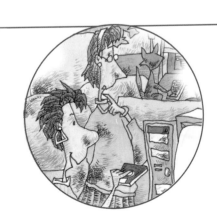

Pair work **B** Practice the conversation with a partner.
Then practice again, using the machines in Get Ready.

3 Listen In

A Look at the words. Which ones could you use to talk about a washing machine? Or a camera?

	1	2	3	4
plug in				
turn on				
open				
press				
put in				
click on				
take out				
turn off				

B Listen and check (✔) the words you hear in each conversation.

C Listen again. Which machine is each person giving instructions for? Number the items (1–4).

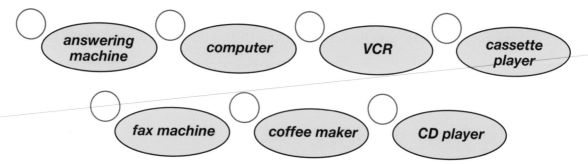

answering machine   computer   VCR   cassette player

fax machine   coffee maker   CD player

4 Say It Right

A Underline the words with the same sound as *s* in *cassette*. Circle the words with the same sound as *sh* in *shirt*.

First, make sure the cord is plugged in.
Next, press the *on* switch. Then you should push
this button. Now, sit back and enjoy the show.
That's all. It's simple.

B Listen and check your answers.

C Listen again and practice.

Try this
We start the first instruction with the word *First*. What other words were used to start other instructions? Can you remember?

First, you turn it on.   65

5 Focus In

A Look at the chart.

Sequencing words	
Do you know how to use a VCR?	Yes, it's easy.
	First, you have to plug it in.
	Next, you need to press the *on* button.
	Now, you put in a tape.
	Finally, you press the *play* button.

B Write the number next to the correct response.

1. What do I do with the lid?   _____ Click the button.
2. What should I do with the power cord?   _____ Just switch it on.
3. What do I have to do with the disk?   _____ Plug it in.
4. How do I start the computer?   _____ You have to put it in here.
5. How do I work the mouse?   _____ You press it down.

C Underline the mistakes. Then write the instructions correctly.

"Well, first you have to plug on the power cord. They you need to turn in the computer. Next, you need to put off a disk. Finally, you have to click out the mouse."

_____

_____

6 Talk Some More

A Write the correct words in the correct spaces.

Spotlight
Uh-huh means *yes* or *I understand.* It is very informal.

Jeff: I can't _____ the VCR.
Sally: Well, first you need to _____ the cord.
Jeff: Oh, OK.
Sally: Then you have to _____ the *on* switch.
Jeff: All right.
Sally: Now, _____ the video tape.
Jeff: Uh-huh.
Sally: Finally, _____ the *play* button.
Jeff: OK. Now what?
Sally: Now, _____ and enjoy the show.

B Check your answers.

Pair work

C Practice the conversation with a partner. Then practice again using different machines.

Work In Pairs   Student A

A Write the correct instruction above each picture. Then use the circles to number the pictures in the correct order (1–4).

- put in a CD
- open the cover
- close the cover
- press the *play* button

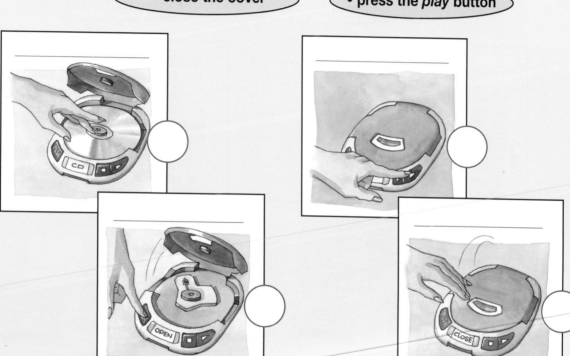

B Read the instructions to your partner. Your partner will write them. Then, ask your partner to tell you which machine you are describing.

Try this

Write some instructions in the wrong order. Put each instruction on a different line. Ask your partner to put your instructions in the correct order.

_____

_____

_____

_____

Work In Pairs — Student B

A Write the correct instruction above each picture. Then use the circles to number the pictures in the correct order (1–4).

- dial the number
- press the *start* button
- put in the paper
- listen for the fax tone

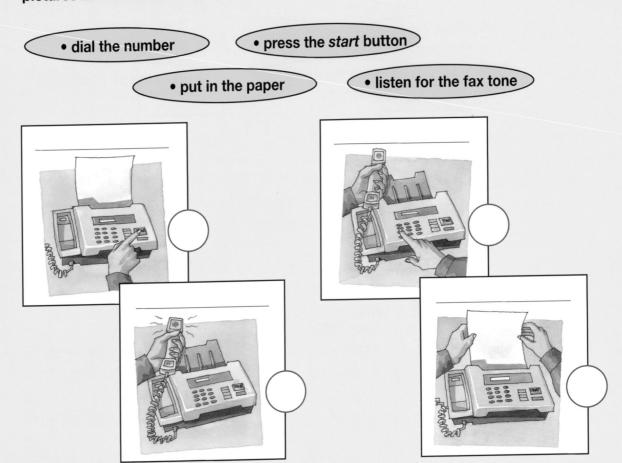

B Read the instructions to your partner. Your partner will write them. Then, ask your partner to tell you which machine you are describing.

Try this

Write some instructions in the wrong order. Put each instruction on a different line. Ask your partner to put your instructions in the correct order.

_____

_____

_____

_____

8 Express Yourself

A Choose one of the machines. Act out the instructions for using it.
Let your partners say which machine you are using.

Group work

B Choose one of the machines in the pictures
and write a list of instructions for it.

9 Think About It

Many companies use recorded
phone messages as part of their
customer service program.
They can be very difficult to understand.

Thank you for calling Century Pizza.
For restaurant locations, press 1.
To hear our complete menu, press 2.
For special promos, press 3.
To place an order, press...

• Do you have a recorded message
on your home telephone? What does it say?

10 Write About It

A Look at the instructions. Number them in the correct order (1–8).

_____ Wait.

_____ Insert the phone card.

_____ Then listen for the dial tone.

_____ Speak when someone answers.

_____ Lift the handset.

_____ Finally, don't forget to take back the phone card!

_____ Put down the handset.

_____ Now punch in the phone number.

B Now write instructions on how to use a fax machine.

First, you turn it on.

• Strategy: Identifying reference words

Who needs an all-electric kitchen?
You can make an oven yourself, using the power of the sun.

Here's how you do it:

You'll need a tall, heavy cardboard box. Cut it as shown and then glue aluminum foil to one side of the cardboard.

Now put your oven in a sunny place, facing the sun. You'll need a large rock to hold up the front panel. If it's windy, you can hold the sides up with more rocks.

Put your food in a black cooking pot. Put the pot on the bottom piece of cardboard. Turn a clear glass bowl upside-down over it.

How does it work? The aluminum foil acts like a mirror. The sunlight hits the foil and reflects off of it. The five foil panels make the sunlight stronger and hotter. You don't have to plug it in or turn it on—the sun does everything for you.

What can you cook? Rice, soup, meat, vegetables—almost anything, but you'll need to double the cooking time. Try it!

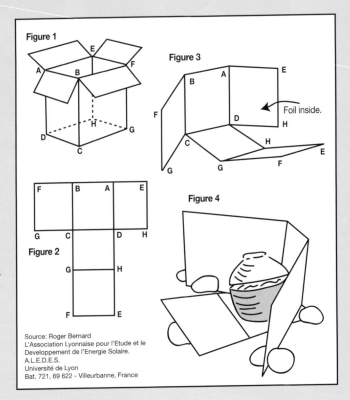

Source: Roger Bernard
L'Association Lyonnaise pour l'Etude et le
Developpement de l'Energie Solaire.
A.L.E.D.E.S.
Université de Lyon
Bat. 721, 69 622 - Villeurbanne, France

**Look at these sentences from the reading passage.
What does the word *it* mean in each one?**

1. How does *it* work?   ___The oven___
2. Cut *it* as shown.   _____
3. Turn a clean glass bowl upside-down over *it*.   _____
4. ... and reflects off of *it*.   _____
5. Try *it*!   _____

Talk About It

◯ Can you cook? What can you cook?

◯ Have you ever cooked outside, maybe on a campfire? What did you make?

◯ Do you like to make things yourself? What did you make?

1 Vocabulary Review

A Which verbs in this unit can you use with *on*, *off*, *in* and *out*?

on	off	in	out

Do you know how to use the VCR?

Yes, it's easy.

2 Grammar Review

A Fill in the blanks.

1. Make sure the cord is plugged _____.

2. Then, you turn it _____.

3. When the song is finished, take _____ the cassette.

4. Click _____ the icon to open the file.

5. After you finish, make sure to turn it _____ again.

B Write instructions on how to operate a VCR using the words shown.

1. (plug in) _____

2. (press) _____

3. (put in) _____

4. (press) _____

5. (sit back) _____

3 Log On

Practice more with the language and topics you studied on the *Expressions* website:

http://expressions.heinle.com

First, you turn it on.

UNIT 9

Goals ....

◑ *Describing routines and schedules*   ◔ *Telling time*

I get up early.

1 Get Ready

A Match the activity with the picture.

1.	start class
2.	take a shower
3.	get up
4.	catch the bus
5.	arrive at school
6.	leave home
7.	make coffee

B Circle the correct answer.

1. What is the opposite of *get up*?
2. What is the opposite of *leave home*?
3. What is the opposite of *arrive at school*?
4. What is the opposite of *class starts*?

Go to bed / Go to sleep

Be home / Come home

Be at school / Leave school

Class finishes / Class stops

2 Start Talking

A Look at the conversation and listen.

Henry: You look tired.

Jane: I am. I'm really busy in the mornings.

Henry: Why?

Jane: Well, I get up at 5:30. I take a shower and
make coffee. Then I leave home at 6:00 and
catch the 6:15 bus. I have to arrive at school
by 7:00. My Spanish class starts at 7:15.

B **Practice with a partner.**
Then practice again using information about your own daily schedule.

3 Listen In

A Look at the activities in the pictures. What time do you think each one happened?

B Listen and number the pictures (1–6).

C What time did each activity happen? Listen again and mark the time on the clocks.

4 Say It Right

A Listen and practice the statement and question intonations.

1. *Five o'clock.*   *Five o'clock?*
2. *Tired.*   *Tired?*
3. *By bus.*   *By bus?*
4. *Busy day.*   *Busy day?*
5. *Downtown.*   *Downtown?*

Try this

I start work AT 9:00. Which two other words (instead of *at*) did you hear before the time in Listen In? Can you remember?

B Listen and circle the best response to each statement you hear.

C Listen again and check your answers.

5 Focus In

A Look at the chart.

Questions with *what + do*	
What do you **do** in the morning?	I **go** to school.
What time does Pete get up?	He **gets up** at around 5:30.
What does she **do** in the evenings?	She **watches** TV or reads a book.
What do they **do** on the weekends?	They **visit** their parents.

B What do you think Sue does at these times? Fill in the blanks.

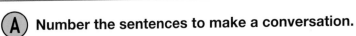

Well, I generally _____ at 6:30.
I _____ and then I have _____ at around 7:30.
I _____ at 8:15. It's a 45-minute trip, so I _____
at around 9:00. I _____ from 12:30–1:30,
and I _____ at 5:00.

C Write five sentences about your own daily schedule.

1. _____
2. _____
3. _____
4. _____
5. _____

6 Talk Some More

Spotlight
How come? is the same as *Why?*, but it is very informal.

A Number the sentences to make a conversation.

Gina: _____ Tired? What time do you get up?

Gina: _____ What's the matter?

Jack: _____ 5:30.

Jack: _____ I'm tired.

Jack: _____ I have an early morning computer class.

Gina: _____ How come?

B Check your answers.

Pair work

C Practice the conversation using the activities on the list in Get Ready.
Then practice again using information about your own daily schedule.

Work In Pairs (Student A)

A Look at the information. What times do you think are missing?

	gets up	has breakfast	goes to work	comes home	has dinner	goes to bed
Matt	6:30 am	_____	7:45 am	_____	7:00 pm	_____
Andrew	_____	5:30 pm	_____	5:15 am	_____	10:00 am

B Ask your partner questions and fill in the missing information.

What time do you get up?

10:30

C What kind of work do you think Andrew does?

D Make up some more times. What time do you think Matt...

takes a shower?   He takes a shower at _____

catches the bus?   He catches the bus at _____

gets to work?   He gets to work at _____

finishes work?   He finishes work at _____

Try this

Now ask your partner for the same information about Andrew. Write four sentences about Andrew with the information.

_____

_____

_____

_____

Work In Pairs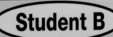

A Look at the information. What times do you think are missing?

	gets up	has breakfast	goes to work	comes home	has dinner	goes to bed
Matt	_____	7:00 am	_____	6:30 pm	_____	10:30 pm
Andrew	5:00 pm	_____	6:00 pm	_____	6:30 am	_____

B Ask your partner questions and fill in the missing information.

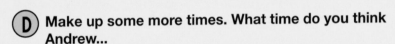

What time do you get up?

10:30

C What kind of work do you think Andrew does?

D Make up some more times. What time do you think Andrew...

takes a shower?   He takes a shower at _____

catches the bus?   He catches the bus at _____

gets to work?   He gets to work at _____

finishes work?   He finishes work at _____

Try this ....

Now ask your partner for the same information about Matt.
Write four sentences about Matt with the information.

_____

_____

_____

_____

8 Express Yourself

A Survey three of your classmates. Find out what time they...

Group work

	Name 1	Name 2	Name 3
get up			
have breakfast			
leave home			
arrive at work or school			
have lunch			
go home			
have dinner			
go to bed			

B Share your information with the class. Then answer these questions.

1. Who gets up the earliest in your class? _____
2. Who gets up the latest? _____
3. Who goes to bed the earliest? _____
4. Who goes to bed the latest? _____

9 *Think About It*

In some cultures it's OK to arrive late for a social event. In other cultures it's important to be on time.

• How about in your culture? Do you have to apologize if you're late?

10 Write About It

A Look at the daily planner.

Mon.
6:15 go jogging
12:00 lunch with Sue
5:30 meet John at Regal theater

Tue.
12:00 meeting with Jerry
1:30 visit clinic
6:30 phone Jim Benson
8:00 meet Phil for drink

Wed.
10:15 pick up photos
1:30 phone dentist
6:45 cocktails with Jen
9:00 dinner with Julie

B Now fill in your own daily schedule.

My Schedule

Mon.	Tue.	Wed.	Thu.	Fri.

Here's a daily routine with a difference...

Lee Weston, Wildlife Biologist, Alaska

I do a lot of work outdoors in the Alaskan mountains. Although it's summer, I have to take snowshoes and a lot of warm clothes. I also take a tent, food, and my backpack.

I sleep in the tent. In summer in Alaska it's always daylight. When I get up I put on warm clothes. I make some breakfast. Then I put on my snowshoes and start work. I'm studying birds. I walk for a certain distance, looking. Then I stand still, writing in my notebook. This goes on all day.

I carry a lot of things: my map, radio, drinking water, lunch and a gun. The gun is for bears. I don't have any bullets in the gun—just noisemakers. I've never used it yet.

It's slow, walking in snowshoes and carrying all that stuff. In early summer the mountain streams are very high with melting snow. Sometimes I have to walk through them. The water is very cold and fast.

For lunch I eat a sandwich, cheese and crackers, and chocolate. Definitely chocolate. Then I work till late at night. I make some dinner and look over my notes. I go to sleep in the daylight, just as I got up.

> **What can you understand from Lee's story? Underline the place in the story where you found the information.**
>
> | | True | False |
> |---|---|---|
> | • Lee sleeps under the stars. | ☐ | ☐ |
> | • She walks in the snow. | ☐ | ☐ |
> | • She likes chocolate. | ☐ | ☐ |
> | • The bears give her a lot of trouble. | ☐ | ☐ |
> | • A stream is like a little river. | ☐ | ☐ |

Talk About It

○ Have you ever camped in a very cold place in the mountains? Talk about it.

○ Lee loves her work. What do you think she likes about it?

○ Do you like working indoors or outdoors? Why?

12 Review

1 Vocabulary Review

A Fill in the blanks with verbs from this unit.

1. _____ a shower.
2. _____ the bus.
3. _____ jogging.
4. _____ work.
5. _____ home.
6. _____ breakfast/lunch/dinner.

B What time do you do these things?

I get up early.
How about you?

2 Grammar Review

A Fill in the blanks.
Then answer the questions with information about your own daily schedule.

1. What time _____ get up?

_____

2. What time _____ have breakfast?

_____

3. What time _____ start English class?

_____

4. What time _____ go to bed?

_____

B Write the correct sentences. Which word is not needed in each sentence?

1. (5:30/I/up/at/get/on) _____ I get up at 5:30. _____ (on)
2. (look/tired/you/matter) _____ ( )
3. (school/he/at/7:00/busy/at/arrives) _____ ( )
4. (I'm/happy/oh/sorry/late) _____ ( )

3 Log On

Practice more with the language and topics you studied on the *Expressions* website:

http://expressions.heinle.com

I'd like a hamburger.

1 Get Ready

A Write the number next to the correct item (1–10).

1. hamburger
2. pizza
3. fries
4. salad
5. chicken
6. hot dog
7. soda
8. iced tea
9. mustard
10. ketchup

B How many toppings can you put on pizza? Make a list and then share it with your partner.

○ Cheese
○ _____
○ _____

○ _____
○ _____
○ _____

2 Start Talking 📼

A Look at the conversation and listen.

Server: Can I help you?

Maxine: I'd like a hamburger and a medium iced tea, please.

Server: Is that all?

Maxine: Yes, thanks.

Pair work **B** Pair work. Practice the conversation with a partner. Practice again ordering different items from the menu.

3 Listen In

(A) Which items in the list could you describe using the word *regular*?

_____ hamburger	_____ hot dog	_____ mustard
_____ fries	_____ soda	_____ ketchup
_____ chicken	_____ coffee	_____ apple
_____ salad	_____ iced tea	_____ pie
_____ pizza	_____ juice	_____ ice cream

(B) Listen and check (✔) the words every time you hear them.

(C) Listen again and take the orders.

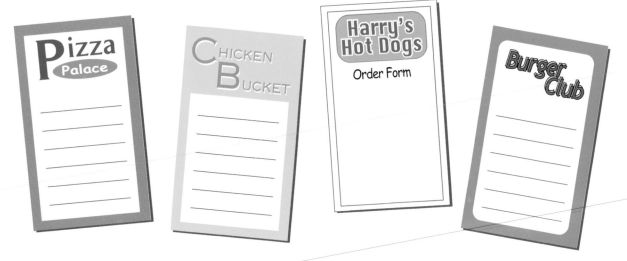

4 Say It Right

(A) Plural (two or more) things end with the letter *s*.
When we are speaking, sometimes the sound is /s/, sometimes the sound is /z/.
Do the words end in /s/ or /z/? Listen and check (✔) the correct column.

	/s/	/z/
drinks	✔	
hamburgers		
hot dogs		
thanks		
napkins		

(B) Listen and check your answers.

(C) Listen again and practice.

Try this.
Choose three words from the list in Listen In.
Do the plural words end with /s/ or /z/?

A Look at the chart.

would like/will have	
Can I help you?	Yes, **I'd like** a cheeseburger please./No, thanks.
Would you like any ketchup and mustard on that?	**I'll have** some ketchup, but I don't want any mustard, thanks.
Would you like a drink?	Yes, **I'll have** an orange juice please.
What size **would you like**?	Small/Medium/Large, please.
Is that all?	Yes, thanks./No, **I'd also like** an iced tea, please.

B Put *some*, *any*, or *a/an* in the blanks. Then practice the conversations with a partner.

A: Can I help you?

B: I'd like _____ hamburger and _____ fries please.

A: Would you like _____ ketchup and mustard on your fries?

B: Yes, can I have _____ mustard, please? Thanks.

C Look at these food items. Fill in the blanks with *some*, *a* or *an*.

1. _____ apple
2. _____ mayonnaise
3. _____ hot dog

4. _____ chicken
5. _____ pizza
6. _____ ice cream cone

6 Talk Some More

A Number the sentences to make a conversation.

Mike: _____ Yes. And a soda, please.

Mike: _____ Yes. Can I have a hamburger, please?

Server: _____ Would you like ketchup and mustard on that?

Server: _____ Can I help you?

Mike: _____ Medium.

Server: _____ What size?

Spotlight
Always say *please* when you want someone to help you!

B Check your answers.

Pair work **C** Practice the conversation with a partner.
Practice again using items from the list in Listen In.

Work In Pairs  Student A

Student B: Use page 84

A Ask your partner for the missing prices of the items on the menu. Write each price in the correct place.

Burger Wizard Menu

Hamburger	regular	.70	double	_____
Cheeseburger	regular	_____	double	1.40
Hot dog	regular	.70	w/cheese	_____
Chicken	regular	_____	large	1.10
French fries	regular	.60	large	_____
Soft drinks	regular	_____	large	.80
Iced tea	regular	.50	large	_____

B Look at the menu and order food from your partner.

C Change roles. You are the server. Practice the conversation again with a new order. Write your partner's order.

Burger Wizard Order Form

Is that all?

Try this

Write down ten prices from the menu above. Say them to your partner and ask for the total. Is your partner's total correct? What is the total?

I'd like a hamburger.

Work In Pairs   Student B

A Ask your partner for the missing prices of the items on the menu.
Write each price in the correct place.

Burger Wizard Menu

Hamburger	regular	_____	double	1.20
Cheeseburger	regular	.90	double	_____
Hot dog	regular	_____	w/cheese	.90
Chicken	regular	.90	large	_____
French fries	regular	_____	large	.80
Soft drinks	regular	.60	large	_____
Iced tea	regular	_____	large	.70

B Imagine you are a server.
Practice taking your partner's order.
Write your partner's order on the order form.

C Now change roles.
Look at the menu
and order food
from your partner.

Is that all?

Burger Wizard Order Form

Try this

Write down ten prices from the menu above. Say them to your partner
and ask for the total. Is your partner's total correct? What is the total?

_____

_____

_____

Express Yourself

A Choose a type of restaurant and create a menu with a partner. Don't forget to list the prices!

Group work

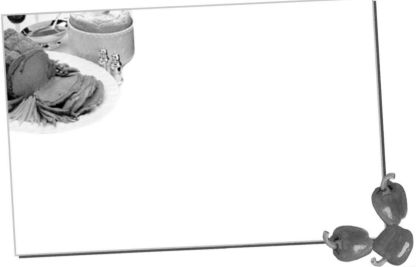

B Work with a different partner. Show your new partner the menu and take the order.

9 *Think About It*

In some cultures, people make special requests when ordering food in a restaurant. In other cultures, people order exactly what is on the menu.

• How about in your culture? Do people usually order extras?

10 Write About It

A Look at the recipe.

B Now write your own favorite recipe.

My Recipe

Recipe

STRAWBERRY SMOOTHIE

Ingredients:
• 10 fresh strawberries
• 1 glass milk
• 2 cups crushed ice

Procedure:
Put all ingredients in a blender. Blend together for 30 seconds. Serve in tall glasses.

• *Strategy: Scanning*

Do you know the origins of these hamburger basics?

Cheese
Most historians believe that cheese originated in the Middle East more than six thousand years ago. The Romans were very good cheesemakers and made many kinds of it. Traders and soldiers spread the idea throughout Europe.

Bread
People began making bread around 12,000 years ago. Around 4,000 years ago the Egyptians began making 'modern' bread with wheat flour and with yeast.

Tomatoes
Early Nahuatl farmers in Mexico planted wild tomatoes for food, so long ago that we don't know when. The English word comes from the Nahuatl word *tomatl*. Travelers from Spain took tomatoes home with them in the 1500s.

Pickles
Cucumbers originated in India a long time ago. They were brought to the Tigris River valley in what is now Iraq. The early Iraqis began to pickle them around 2030 B.C. The Egyptians and Romans also enjoyed pickles.

Potatoes
Potatoes were first grown in the Andes Mountains of South America. Spanish travelers took them back home in the 16th century. From there, they spread to Europe and North America.

Write the names and the dates of the foods in the places where they originated. If the reading has no information, write *don't know*.

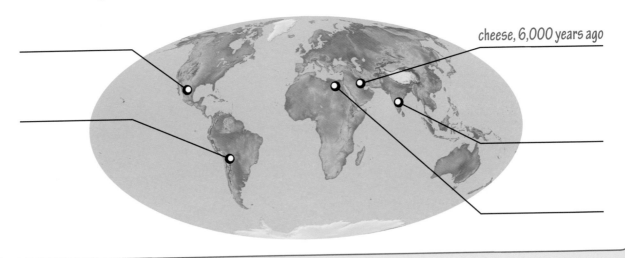

cheese, 6,000 years ago

Talk About It

○ What's your favorite fast food?

○ What international fast foods are popular where you live?

○ What fast foods from your country are popular in other countries?

12 Review

1 Vocabulary Review

A Fill in the chart with words you learned in this unit.

Food	Drink	Size

B Which of the foods in the chart do you often eat?

2 Grammar Review

A Fill in the blanks.

1. _____ _____ help you?
2. _____ _____ have a hot dog, please?
3. _____ _____ like mustard and ketchup on that?
4. _____ _____ all?
5. _____ also like an iced tea, please.

What size would you like?

Large, please.

B Make sentences using the words shown.

1. (hamburger/fries) _____
2. (regular/hot dog) _____
3. (like/mustard) _____
4. (size/like) _____
5. (salad/without) _____

3 Log On

Practice more with the language and topics you studied on the *Expressions* website:

http://expressions.heinle.com

I'd like a hamburger.

○ *Inviting*   ○ *Making excuses*

Do you want to see a movie?

1 Get Ready

A Look at the picture.
What types of movies
can you see on the posters?
Write the number
in the correct place.

1. science fiction
2. comedy
3. thriller
4. drama
5. action film

B Think of two real movie titles for each category below. Write them in the spaces.

1. science fiction _____
2. comedies _____
3. thrillers _____
4. dramas _____
5. action films _____

2 Start Talking

A Look at the conversation and listen.

Alice: Do you want to see a movie?
Rob: Which one?
Alice: How about *Arrival of the Visitors*?
Rob: Oh, no. I don't like science fiction.

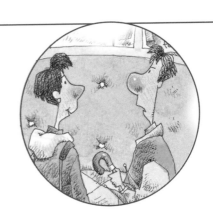

Pair work

B Practice the conversation with a partner.
Then practice again using different movies.

3 Listen In

A Which types of movies can you see in the pictures below?

B Listen and match the theater with the type of movie.

C Why can't the people go to the movies tonight?
Listen again and write the number of the excuse next to the correct movie.

1. I'm going out with Judy.   **3.** I have to work late.

2. I have to study.   **4.** I'm going to the ball game.

4 Say It Right

A Listen to the intonation and
check (✔) the responses that show surprise.

1. _____ You do? That's too bad.
2. _____ You are, huh? Well, maybe next time.
3. _____ You can't? Oh, that's too bad.
4. _____ He is? I didn't know that.
5. _____ She can't. She has to study.

B Listen again and practice.

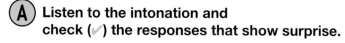

Try this...

What statements do you think went before the surprise responses? Write them. Then practice making the statements and giving surprise responses with a partner.

5 Focus In

(A) Look at the chart.

I'm _____ing and I have to	
What **are** you **doing** tonight?	**I'm going** to the movies.
What **are** your friends **doing** this weekend?	**They're going** to the beach.
Do you want to see the new sci fi movie?	I can't. **I'm going** to a concert.
How about going on a picnic?	I can't. **I have to** study.
What's Pete up to this evening?	**He has to** work late.

(B) Number the sentences to make a conversation. Then practice with a partner.

_____ I can't, Sally. I have to go to a meeting.   _____ Which one?

_____ It's a thriller called *The Knife*.   _____ Hi, John.

_____ Do you want to see a movie?   _____ Hi, Sally.

(C) Fill in the blanks using *have to* or _____ing.

1. I can't go to the ball game. I _____ (finish) my homework.
2. I _____ (visit) my sick aunt in the hospital.
3. They _____ (work late) tonight.
4. We _____ (pick up) our parents and then _____ (take) them to dinner.
5. He _____ (study) and then he _____ (take) his girlfriend to the movies.

6 Talk Some More

Spotlight
It's usually best to start your excuse with the word *Sorry*.

(A) Number the sentences to make a conversation (1–6).

Carol: _____ Oh, no. I forgot. I have to work late tonight.

Pete: _____ Do you want to go to a concert tonight?

Pete: _____ The Screamers.

Carol: _____ Hi, Pete.

Carol: _____ Who's playing?

Pete: _____ Hello, Carol.

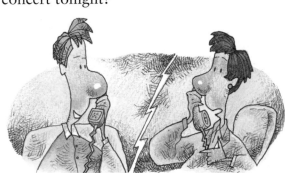

(B) Check your answers.

Pair work **(C)** Practice the conversation with a partner.
Then practice again using your own information.

Work In Pairs Student A

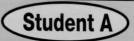

A Look at the activities in the chart.
Which are related to work and which are not?

	Friday Evening	Saturday Afternoon	Saturday Evening	Sunday Afternoon	Sunday Evening
Bob	work late	_____	meet boss at airport	_____	prepare for a meeting
Karen	_____	free	_____	go shopping	_____
Philip	free	_____	free	_____	free
Joan	_____	take car to garage	_____	bake cookies	_____

B You and your partner want to go and
see a movie with your friends.
Ask questions and decide the best time to go.

How about Friday evening for Bob?

He has to work late.

C Change one thing about each person's schedule. Do the exercise again.

Try this

Why can't Bob go to the movies on Friday, Saturday and Sunday evenings?
Write his excuses.

○ Because_____

○ Because_____

○ Because_____

Work In Pairs   Student B

(A) Look at the activities in the chart.
Which are related to work and which are not?

	Friday Evening	Saturday Afternoon	Saturday Evening	Sunday Afternoon	Sunday Evening
Bob	_____	go to meeting	_____	free	_____
Karen	clean apartment	_____	visit aunt in hospital	_____	free
Philip	_____	play tennis	_____	study for exam	_____
Joan	free	_____	go to concert	_____	free

(B) You and your partner want to go and
see a movie with your friends.
Ask questions and decide the best time to go.

How about Friday evening for Karen?

She has to clean her apartment.

(C) Change one thing about each person's schedule. Do the exercise again.

Try this

Why can't Bob go to the movies on Friday, Saturday and Sunday evenings?
Write his excuses.

○ Because_____

○ Because_____

○ Because_____

8 Express Yourself

(A) Make a note of the things you have to do this week. Leave two spaces free.

	Monday	Tuesday	Wednesday	Thursday	Friday
Afternoon					
Evening					

Group work

(B) Talk to your partners and arrange a time to see a movie. You might need to change your schedule.

9 Think About It

In English-speaking cultures, if someone invites you out but you can't go, you should give a reason why. If you're doing something you *want to* do, you say *I'm...* If it's something you *don't want to* do, you say *I have to...*

- How about in your culture? Do you give reasons? What do you say?

10 Write About It

(A) Look at the invitation and the replies.

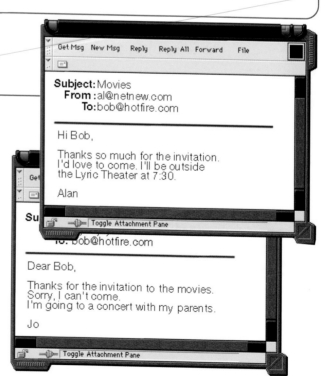

Get Msg New Msg Reply Reply All Forward File

Subject: Movies
From : al@netnew.com
To: bob@hotfire.com

Hi Bob,

Thanks so much for the invitation. I'd love to come. I'll be outside the Lyric Theater at 7:30.

Alan

Get Msg New Msg Reply Reply All Forward File

Subject: Movies
From : bob@hotfire.com
To: jojo@joynet.com
al@netnew.com

Dear Alan and Jo,

Do you want to come to the movies tomorrow night? There's a new science fiction movie showing at the Lyric Theater.

Bob

Toggle Attachment Pane

To: bob@hotfire.com

Dear Bob,

Thanks for the invitation to the movies. Sorry, I can't come. I'm going to a concert with my parents.

Jo

Toggle Attachment Pane

(B) Now write your own invitation to a movie or a concert on a piece of paper and pass it to several students. They will write a note accepting or rejecting the invitation.

• *Strategy: Inferring vocabulary*

What's the latest thing in movies?
It's called digital filmmaking, or desktop filmmaking.

All you need is a digital camcorder, a computer, and some special software. These cost about US$6,000. After you have the equipment, you can make a full-length movie for less than US$1,000.

Think about it. You can tell your own story. Use the camcorder to shoot in your house, in your favorite park, on a bus. When you finish, you can look at your 'takes' immediately on the computer. Edit them any way you like. Keep the best ones, 'cut' the bad ones.

This is the way of the future. Homemade movies are hot right now. Do you want to check it out? Do a web search for 'desktop filmmaking,' or 'digital filmmaking.' You can learn how to do it and where to buy the equipment.

What could be more fun than getting together with a bunch of friends and making your own movie?

Find a word or expression in the text that means the same as

1. a video camera   (1 word) _____
2. the things that you need   (1 word) _____
3. choose the best 'shots' for the movie   (1 word) _____
4. popular   (1 word) _____
5. look at it   (3 words) _____

Talk About It

○ What's your favorite movie? What do you like about it?

○ Do you like the idea of independent, homemade movies? Why or why not?

○ Where would be a good place to make a video? Why?

12 Review

1 Vocabulary Review

A Unscramble the words to make film types.

1. INOCAT _____action_____
2. AMRAD _____
3. RITHRELL _____
4. MEYDOC _____
5. RORRHO _____

Do you want to go out on Thursday?

I'm sorry, I can't. I'm...

B What are *your* favorite types of movies?

2 Grammar Review

A Fill in the blanks with the correct excuses.

1. Do you want to see a movie?

I'm sorry, _____ (do my homework).

I'm sorry, _____ (go to a concert).

2. Do you want to go out tonight?

I'm sorry, _____ (meet my friend).

I'm sorry, _____ (wash my car).

3. How about going out for lunch?

I'm sorry, _____ (finish this report).

I'm sorry, _____ (go on a picnic).

B Make a conversation using the words shown.

hello/Bob/Susan/want/concert/who/the Boston Pops/sorry/work late tonight

_____

_____

_____

_____

3 Log On

Practice more with the language and topics you studied on the *Expressions* website:

http://expressions.heinle.com

Do you want to see a movie? **95**

Goals

○ *Talking about the weather* ○ *Making suggestions*

What's the weather like?

1 Get Ready

A Write the number of the adjectives next to the correct picture.

1.	hot
2.	snowy
3.	cold
4.	sunny
5.	rainy
6.	cloudy
7.	fine

B What are the opposites? Write each one in the correct space.

(**cold**) (**wet**) (**low**) (**cool**) (**rainy**) (**cloudy**)

1. hot _____   4. fine _____
2. warm _____   5. high _____
3. sunny _____   6. dry _____

2 Start Talking

A Look at the conversation and listen.

Murray: What's the weather like there?
Sue: It's hot and sunny.
Murray: Oh, really? It's cold and snowy here.

Pair work

B Practice the conversation with a partner. Practice again using different adjectives.

3 Listen In

A Which words do you think you might hear in a weather forecast? Circle them.

> later   next year   this afternoon
>
> last month   tomorrow   right now

B Listen to the weather reports. Which ones describe the weather now? Which ones give a forecast? Circle *yes* or *no*.

	1	**2**	**3**	**4**
Now	yes/no	yes/no	yes/no	yes/no
Forecast	yes/no	yes/no	yes/no	yes/no

C Listen again. Check (✔) the words you hear in each report.

	1	2	3	4
hot				
cold				
rainy				
fine				
snowy				
sunny				
cloudy				

Let's go to the beach on Saturday.

I don't think that's a very good idea.

4 Say It Right

A Listen to the examples. Which is more important—the weather or the time?

B Listen and check (✔) the correct column.

C Listen again and practice.

Try this

Listen again. On a separate piece of paper, try writing the sentences.

	Weather	**Time**
Example 1	✔	
Example 2		✔
1.		
2.		
3.		
4.		
5.		

5 Focus In

(A) Look at the chart.

Let's and *going to*

What's the weather like?	It's hot and sunny.
What's the weather **going to** be like?	It's **going to** be cloudy.
What are you **going to** do on the weekend?	I'm not sure—maybe I'll play tennis.
Let's go on a picnic.	That sounds like a good idea.
Let's go to a ball game.	No, I don't think it's a good idea.

(B) Fill in the blanks to make conversations.

A: _____'s go to the beach tomorrow.
B: What's the weather _____ to be like?
A: It's going _____ fine.
B: That _____ a good idea.

A: What _____ you _____ do this weekend?
B: I'm not sure—maybe I'll _____ shopping.
A: _____ sounds like a good idea.
   Can I come with you?
B: Sure. _____ go together.

(C) Write the number of the sentence next to the best response.

1. Let's go hiking this summer.
2. What's the weather like there?
3. Let's go to a ball game tonight.
4. What are you going to do tomorrow?
5. What's the weather going to be like?

_____ It's cold and wet.
_____ Sorry, I can't. I have to study this evening.
_____ It's going to be sunny, I think.
_____ That sounds like a good idea. I like mountains.
_____ I'm not sure—maybe I'll stay home.

6 Talk Some More

Spotlight
Let's... is an easy way to make a suggestion. You can also use *Why don't we...?*

(A) Write the words in the correct spaces.

(tomorrow)   (OK)   (what's)   (hot and sunny)

Julia: Let's go on a picnic _____.
 Jeff: _____ the weather going to be like?
Julia: It's going to be _____.
 Jeff: _____. That sounds like a good idea.

(B) Check your answers.

Pair work **(C)** Practice the conversation with a partner.
Then practice again using your own information.

Work In Pairs   Student A

A Read the statements to your partner. Your partner will tell you if it's a good idea or not.

- *It's going to be rainy tomorrow. Let's go on a picnic.*
- *It's going to be rainy tomorrow. Let's stay in.*
- *It's going to be sunny tomorrow. Let's go to the park.*

B Suggest the following activities to your partner. Your partner will comment.

Thursday	Friday	Saturday	Sunday
Baseball: Sluggers play against the Swingers at the Laredo open-air stadium. 7:00 pm	**Outdoor Concert:** Whispering Children on tour. At the music hall. 8:00 pm	**Movies:** *Ships on the Horizon* opens at the Bel-Air Cinema. 7:15 & 9:15 pm	**Garden Shows:** Rose exhibit at the Cultural Center Park. One day only. 10:00 am– 8:00 pm

C Which activities are you going to do together?

Let's go on a picnic tomorrow.

Well...

What's the weather going to be like?

Try this

Think of two outdoor and two indoor activities. Suggest them to a partner. Write a conversation and practice it with your partner.

_____

_____

_____

_____

What's the weather like?   **99**

Work In Pairs (Student B)

A Read the statements to your partner. Your partner will tell you if it's a good idea or not.

- *It's going to be cloudy tomorrow. Let's sunbathe.*
- *It's going to be snowy tomorrow. Let's go to the beach.*
- *It's going to be snowy tomorrow. Let's make a snowman.*

B Listen to your partner's suggestions. Look at the weather forecast and give answers.

Thursday	Friday	Saturday	Sunday
AM ☀	**AM** ☁	**AM** ☁	**AM** 🌧→☁
PM ☁→🌧	**PM** ☀	**PM** ☁	**PM** ☀

C Which activities are you going to do together?

Let's go on a picnic tomorrow.

Well...

What's the weather going to be like?

Try this

Think of two outdoor and two indoor activities. Suggest them to a partner. Write a conversation and practice it with your partner.

_____

_____

_____

_____

8 Express Yourself

(A) Write weather forecasts for a famous capital city. Do not say where it is.

Tomorrow	Next Month	In Six Months
_____	_____	_____
_____	_____	_____
_____	_____	_____
_____	_____	_____

Group work

(B) Take turns reading your forecasts. The group will try to guess which city it is.

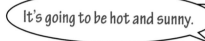
It's going to be hot and sunny.

9 Think About It

In many cultures, the weather is a popular topic of conversation.

- How about in your culture? Do people talk about the weather?
- What other topics of small talk are common?

10 Write About It

(A) Look at the weather forecasts.

Pleasantville	☀	High 27 Low 16	Blue skies: warm and sunny.
High Plains	☁	High 15 Low 4	Cool to cold with cloudy skies. Rain later.
Winchester	⛅	High 23 Low 9	Some morning clouds. Afternoon sunny. Showers again at night.

(B) On a separate piece of paper, make up a forecast for your city tomorrow.

Perfect Weather For Polar Bears

• *Strategy: Skimming*

Have you heard of Polar Bear Clubs?
Every January 1, their members celebrate the new year.
How? By going swimming in a freezing-cold river or lake!

This is the story of the Jacksonport Polar Bear Club (JPBC) in the United States.

It started in 1987 with a young boy named J.R. Jarosh. He jumped into Lake Michigan. The air temperature that day was -6°C, but J.R. went swimming anyway. He did the same thing for the next two years. In 1990, two more brave people joined him. Then the following year there were twelve. In 2000, six hundred people jumped into the freezing lake. And once again, J.R. Jarosh was one of them.

On the JPBC website, J.R. offers some important advice for future Polar Bears. He has learned all this from experience. He says they should wear shoes to protect their feet from the ice. They should bring warm boots to put on after swimming. And they should bring a blanket to sit on.

Answer the questions:

1. Who is this passage about? _____
2. What do they do every year? _____
3. Where do they do it? _____
4. What day do they do it? _____
5. What advice do they follow? _____

Talk About It

○ Why do you think people go swimming in freezing weather?
○ Do you think they are strange? Why or why not?
○ What kind of strange things do people do in your country?

 **Review**

1 Vocabulary Review

A Fill in the chart with words you learned in this unit.

Good Weather	Bad Weather

B What's your favorite kind of weather? Why?

What's the weather the weather going to be like tomorrow?

Maybe it'll be sunny!

2 Grammar Review

A Fill in the blanks.

1. _____ go to the beach.
2. _____ the weather going to be like?
3. Oh! _____ going to be cloudy and rainy.
4. I don't think _____ a good idea.

B Look back to Work In Pairs, Student B.
Write the weather forecast for Thursday and Friday.

On Thursday morning, it's going to be sunny. _____

_____

_____

_____

3 Log On

Practice more with the language and topics you studied on the *Expressions* website:

http://expressions.heinle.com

Goals

○ *Talking about what people like*   ○ *Talking about gift giving*

What can we get him?

Get Ready

A **Look at the gifts in the list. Write the number next to the correct picture.**

> **1.** a ticket to San Francisco
> **2.** some chocolates
> **3.** a tennis racket
> **4.** flowers
> **5.** a book
> **6.** some music

B **What gifts could you buy someone who likes music? Or travel? Make two lists.**

Music	Travel

Start Talking

A **Look at the conversation and listen.**

> **Alex:** Max is leaving on Friday. What can we get him?
> **Gina:** I don't know. What does he like?
> **Alex:** Well, he likes music. Let's get him a CD.
> **Gina:** Great idea. I'm sure he'll like that.

Pair work **B** **Practice the conversation with a partner.**
Than practice again using different names, likes and gifts.

3 Listen In

A Listen and write each person's likes and interests in the chart.

	likes/interests	suggested gift
Julian		
Annie		
John		
Sandy		

B Listen again and write the gifts people suggest in the chart above.

C Choose the best gift for each person. Write the person's name under the gift.

Fitness Club — FITNESS CENTER — MEMBER

GIFT CERTIFICATE $20 — Read More Bookstore

World Class Entertainment Presents
Einstein Symphony Orchestra Concert
Seat No. G 661   8:00pm Tuesday August 22

Einstein Symphony Orchestra Concert

An Invitation
Aunt Martha's Garden Show
Featuring Rare Orchids
Chrysanthemums, Marigolds, Hyacinths and many more
Open Daily
September 10–30

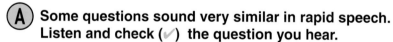

4 Say It Right

A Some questions sound very similar in rapid speech.
Listen and check (✔) the question you hear.

1. _____ What's he like?   _____ What does he like?
2. _____ What's he like?   _____ What does he like?
3. _____ What's she like?   _____ What does she like?
4. _____ What's she like?   _____ What does she like?
5. _____ What's she like?   _____ What does she like?

Try this

Try saying the questions. Speak as quickly as you can. Your partner will answer. Was the answer correct?

B Listen again and check your answers.

C Listen again and practice.

5 Focus In

A Look at the chart.

Let's/how about...? and like	
What do you **like**?	I **like** pop music.
What does she **like** doing?	She **likes** playing football.
Let's get her a CD.	Great idea! She'll **like** that.
How about getting her a cookbook?	No, she already has a lot of cookbooks.

B Fill in the blanks to make four conversations.

A: It's Cathy's birthday. What can we get her?
B: _____ buy her a CD.

A: What do Bob and Gina like?
B: _____ movies.

A: What should we get Geoff for his birthday?
B: _____ getting him a new watch?

A: What does your brother like doing?
B: _____ playing golf.

C Suggest gifts for these people. Use *Let's* or *How about...?*

1. Ahmed likes reading. Let's get him a book. _____
2. Maria likes hiking. _____
3. Jenny likes music. _____
4. Steve likes flowers. _____

6 Talk Some More

A Write the words in the correct spaces.

likes *getting* *has*
like *get*

Alex: It's Jo's birthday next week. I don't know what to _____ her.
Gina: What does she _____?
Alex: She _____ cooking
Gina: How about _____ her a cookbook?
Alex: No, she already _____ a lot of cookbooks.

B Check your answers.

Pair work

C Practice the conversation with a partner.
Then practice again using other people you both know.

> **Spotlight**
> We can also say *What about...?* instead of *How about...?*

Work In Pairs  Student A

Student B: Use page 108

A Look at the information below. Describe what Bill likes to your partner.
Your partner will suggest gifts for Bill. Decide which suggestions are good.

Bill likes...

He already has a lot of...
cookbooks
tennis balls
videos

B Listen to your partner and note down the things Connie likes.
Suggest some gifts for Connie. Make a list of suggested gifts in the chart.

Connie likes...	Suggestions

C Decide with your partner which gifts you should get for Bill and Connie.

Try this

Which of the suggested gifts above would *you* like to receive? Why?

_____

_____

Work In Pairs (Student B)

Student A: Use page 107

A Listen to your partner and note down the things Bill likes.
Suggest some gifts for Bill. Make a list of suggested gifts in the chart.

Bill likes...	Suggestions

B Look at the information below. Describe what Connie likes to your partner.
Your partner will suggest gifts for Connie. Decide which suggestions are good.

Connie likes...

She already has a lot of...
workout clothes
art books
classical music CDs

C Decide with your partner which gifts you should get for Bill and Connie.

Try this

Which of the suggested gifts above would *you* like to receive? Why?

_____

_____

Express Yourself

A Write three hobbies or activities that you like.

My hobbies/activities

What do you like doing?

Group work

B Ask each person in your group what they like to do.
Decide the best gift for each person.

Think About It

Oh, how sweet of you!

Oh, you shouldn't have.

Each culture has its own traditions about when you should give gifts, what you should give, and what to do and say when you get a gift.

• What are the traditions in your culture?

Write About It

A Look at the thank you note.

B Think of a gift you received in the past.
Now write a note thanking the person for the gift.

Thank You!

Dear David,
Thank you so much for the electronic currency calculator. It's just what I wanted! I'm sure it will be very useful on my trip to Singapore.
Chris

The Best Presents to Give

• Strategy: Reading actively

Read these statements. Then read the article to decide if the statements are *True* or *False*.

	True	False
• The Chinese never give knives.	☐	☐
• Chinese clocks are dangerous.	☐	☐
• Two is good in Hong Kong but bad in Russia.	☐	☐
• Red roses mean romance in Germany.	☐	☐
• Two is bad in Russia and Germany.	☐	☐

Gift-giving Rules Around the World

Hong-Shin Wei, Hong Kong

You must never give a clock to a Chinese person, because the sound of the word for 'clock' is similar to the word for 'death' in Chinese. Also, don't wrap a gift in white, black, or blue paper, because these are the colors for funerals. Don't give a knife, because something sharp can cut a relationship.

Eugen Karpenko, Russia

If we give flowers as a gift, we have to give an odd number of them (one, three, five, etc.) because even numbers of flowers (two, four, six, etc.) are for funerals. If we give a gift of alcohol and the host opens it, we should empty it together. And we should always toast the bottle before we take a drink.

Rosie Kuhlmann, Germany

Flowers are a good gift to take to your dinner hostess, but don't take her red roses because it means you are in love with her. Don't take thirteen of anything because it's an unlucky number. Don't take an even number of anything, either. Don't wrap your gift in white, brown, or black paper.

Talk About It

○ Which of these gift-giving customs are the same in your culture?

○ Which times of the year do you give gifts?

○ Do you give special types of gifts at weddings? What?

12 Review

1 Vocabulary Review

A Fill in the chart with as many gifts as you can think of for people who like sports, music and travel.

Sports	Music	Travel

B What's the best gift you ever received?

How about getting him some shoes?

2 Grammar Review

A Fill in the blanks with the correct form of the verb.

It's Jo's birthday next week.

How about (*get*) _____ her some flowers?

What about (*buy*) _____ her a CD?

Let's (*give*) _____ her a gift certificate.

Sophia's leaving on Friday.

How about (*buy*) _____ her a backpack?

Let's (*get*) _____ her a computer game.

What about (*give*) _____ her a watch?

B Suggest gifts for these people.

1. Bill likes soccer. _____

2. Marie likes pop music. _____

3. Aya likes traveling. _____

4. Stephan likes studying. _____

3 Log On

Practice more with the language and topics you studied on the *Expressions* website:

http://expressions.heinle.com

UNIT 14

Goals

○ *Making suggestions*   ○ *Voicing objections*

We should go to the beach.

1 **Get Ready**

(A) **Look at the sentences and number the pictures (1–5).**

1. It's too hot.
2. I don't like hiking.
3. It's too expensive.
4. We don't speak Spanish.
5. It's too far.

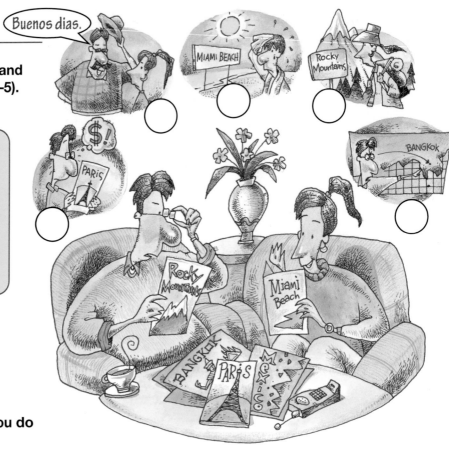

Buenos dias.

(B) **What activities could you do in these places?**

Bangkok _____   Miami   _____
Paris   _____   Mexico City _____

2 **Start Talking**

(A) **Look at the conversation and listen.**

Dennis: Where should we go on vacation?
Renee: I think we should go to the beach.
Dennis: No, it's too hot. I think we should go hiking.
Renee: But I don't like hiking.

Pair work (B) **Practice the conversation with a partner.**
Practice again using the other places in Get Ready.

112

3 Listen In

A Look at the *Things To Do* in the chart. Where would you go for these things? Check your ideas with your partner.

B Listen and write the names of the places Rick suggests.

Place	Things To Do	Objection
• _____	• hiking	• *too expensive*
• _____	• temples, markets	• *don't speak Spanish*
• _____	• museums, food, nightclubs	• *too far*
• _____	• galleries, shopping	• *don't like hiking*

C Listen again and match the places, things to do and objections.

Try this
What one word does the man use to begin a new suggestion? Can you remember?

Where should we go tomorrow?

I think we should go shopping.

4 Say It Right

A The words *can* and *can't* often sound very similar. But their meanings are exactly opposite! Listen and circle the words you hear.

1. I **can / can't** swim.
2. I **can / can't** go in July.
3. We **can / can't** afford it.
4. They **can / can't** speak Spanish.
5. She **can / can't** meet us at Christmas.

B Listen again and check your answers.

C Listen again and practice.

Try this
Write down five things you can or can't do. Tell your partner.

We should go to the beach.   **113**

5 Focus In

(A) Look at the chart.

Can and *should*

Can you swim?	Yes, I **can.**/No, I **can't.**
Can Maria speak English?	Yes, she **can.**/No, she **can't.**
What **can** we do at the beach?	We **can** go swimming.
Where **should** we go on vacation?	We **should** go to the beach.

(B) Fill in the blanks. Use the words *should*, *can*, or *can't*.
Then practice the conversations with another student.

A: We _____ go to the beach.
B: But I _____ swim.

A: Where _____ we go on vacation?
B: Maybe we _____ go hiking.
A: That's a good idea.

(C) Can you _____? Fill in the blanks with *yes* or *no*. Then make complete sentences.

1. __No__ lift 1000 kg.   I can't lift 1000 kg. _____
2. _____ tap dance   _____
3. _____ speak Turkish   _____
4. _____ play the guitar   _____
5. _____ cook   _____
6. _____ paint pictures   _____

6 Talk Some More

(A) Number the sentences to make a conversation (1–5).

Jim: _____ I think we should go to the beach.
Jim: _____ We can go swimming.
Julie: _____ What can we do there?
Julie: _____ But I don't like swimming.
Julie: _____ Where should we go on vacation?

Spotlight
Instead of *I think we should*, we can also say *Why don't we...?*

(B) Check your answers.

Pair work **(C)** Practice the conversation with a partner.
Practice again suggesting different places to go.

114   Unit 14

Work In Pairs — Student A

A What things do you think you could do in Italy? Make a list.

B Look at the brochure. When your partner asks you, suggest a vacation in Singapore. Tell your partner about the things you can do there.

Singapore

Visit the Night Safari for a close-up view of the animal kingdom.

Enjoy exotic flavors from a variety of cultures.

Botanical gardens delight visitors all year long.

Orchard Road—a shopper's paradise known around the world.

C Your partner has some information about Italy. Ask what you can do there. Say which suggestions you like and which you don't.

Decide together which place is best for you.

Try this

Write two sentences about the country you are both going to visit and what you are going to do there.

We are going to visit...

We should go to the beach.   **115**

Work In Pairs (**Student B**)

A **What things do you think you could do in Singapore? Make a list.**

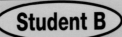

Where should we go on our vacation?

Maybe Singapore would be nice.

B **Your partner has some information about Singapore.**
Ask what you can do there. Say which suggestions you like and which you don't.

Italy's design houses tempt fashion lovers.

Italy's historical sites attract millions each year.

Discover a rich variety of cuisine.

Works of the great masters delight art lovers.

Italy

C **Look at the brochure above. When your partner asks you, suggest a vacation in Italy. Tell your partner about the things you can do there.**

Decide together which place is best for you.

Try this

Write two sentences about the country you are both going to visit and what you are going to do there.

We are going to visit...

_____

8 Express Yourself

(A) Choose a vacation spot anywhere in the world. Brainstorm a list of things to do there.

Destination: _____

Group work →

Activities
_____
_____
_____
_____

I really need a vacation!

(B) Talk to students from other groups. Who would like to come to your vacation spot?

9 *Think About It*

Different cultures have different ideas about how much time we should spend on vacation.

- How about in your country? What is the usual length of time?
- What are the most popular vacation spots?

10 Write About It

(A) Look at the tour brochure for London.

London London is an exciting city. It has many superb areas for sightseeing.

Cruise down the River Thames to historic Greenwich.

Visit the Houses of Parliament and Westminster Abbey.

Go inside Big Ben, the world's most famous clock tower.

Travel around the city is easy and cheap—on a double decker bus.

London has something to offer visitors of all ages!

(B) On a piece of paper make a tour brochure for your own city or area.

11 Read On | Three All-American Roads

• *Strategy: Inferring content*

Read the article. Then read the statements and answer *True* or *False*.

	True	False
• There are many hotels on the Natchez Trace Parkway.	☐	☐
• All of these roads have natural beauty.	☐	☐
• All of the roads have historical places.	☐	☐
• You can go shopping on the Columbia River Highway.	☐	☐
• The San Juan Skyway offers the most activities.	☐	☐

The United States government has named 20 roads 'All-American Roads.' These roads are especially natural or historical.

The Natchez Trace Parkway

About 200 years ago, today's Parkway was just a trail. People walked or rode horses. They slept on the ground. They carried their food with them. Sometimes robbers stole everything they had. They had to watch out for snakes, insects and wild animals. Today, a lovely road follows the old trail. There are no trucks, no shops or businesses—just forests and fields.

The Columbia River Highway

This little road goes through the mountains above the Columbia River, which is one of the largest rivers in the United States. The road passes many waterfalls. You can park and walk through the forest to the falls. There are lots of wildflowers in the spring. It's a wonderful place for a picnic. Don't forget your camera!

The San Juan Skyway

This road feels like the roof of the world. You drive very high, through the beautiful Rocky Mountains. You pass through little historic towns. The views of the mountaintops and the long valleys are amazing. You can see very old ruins of American Indian civilizations. You can stop to hike, camp, bicycle, fish, shop. Come in the autumn and see the golden leaves.

Talk About It

○ Which road do you think you would enjoy the most? Why?

○ Have you ever taken a trip on an interesting road? Talk about it.

○ What's your idea of a perfect vacation?

1 Vocabulary Review

A Make a list of vacation places and activities you learned in this unit.
Can you add any more?

Vacation places

_____
_____
_____
_____

Vacation activities

_____
_____
_____
_____

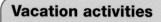

We should go to Japan on vacation.

B What are you going to do for your next vacation?

2 Grammar Review

A Complete the questions with *Can*, *What* or *Where*.
Then write the number of the question next to the best response.

1. _____ you dance?
2. _____ can we do in Paris?
3. _____ should we go on vacation?
4. _____ Leo speak Japanese?
5. _____ should we get Amy for her birthday?

_____ Well, we can go shopping.
_____ Let's go to Mexico.
_____ No, I can't.
_____ Let's get her some flowers.
_____ Yes, he can.

B Write four activities which visitors can do in your country.

1. _____
2. _____
3. _____
4. _____

3 Log On

Practice more with the language and topics you studied on the *Expressions* website:

http://expressions.heinle.com

Goals

○ Describing people and jobs　　○ Using degrees of description

What's she like?

1 Get Ready

A The scrambled words in the picture are adjectives to describe people's personal qualities. Unscramble them and write them in the spaces.

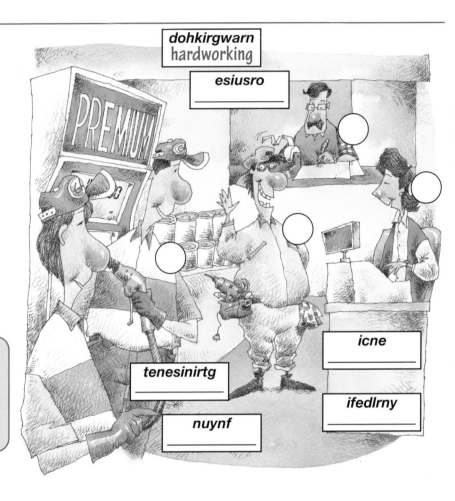

dohkirgwarn
hardworking

esiusro
_____

icne
_____

tenesinirtg
_____

nuynf
_____

ifedlrny
_____

B Write the number of each job in the correct place in the picture (1–4).

1. cashier
2. manager
3. mechanic
4. pump attendant

2 Start Talking

A Look at the conversation and listen.

Dario:　Did you meet the new cashier?
Mario:　No, I didn't. What's she like?
Dario:　Oh, she's really nice.
Mario:　Really? I think I'll go and say 'hello.'

Pair work

B Practice the conversation with a partner.
Then practice again, using different jobs and different adjectives.

3 Listen In

A Which of the adjectives below describe *you*? Can you add more?

(nice)   (friendly)   (hardworking)

(serious)   (interesting)   (funny)

B Listen. Who are the people in the conversations talking about?
Number the pictures (1–4).

C Listen again. Draw lines to match the people with the descriptions above.

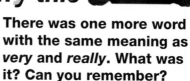

Try this

There was one more word with the same meaning as *very* and *really*. What was it? Can you remember?

4 Say It Right

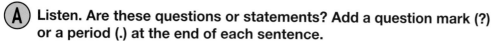

A Listen. Are these questions or statements? Add a question mark (?) or a period (.) at the end of each sentence.

1. Your boss is really funny
2. My job is kind of boring
3. The new receptionist is extremely nice
4. Her sister's really serious
5. Your job is boring

B Listen again and check your answers.

C Listen again and practice.

Try this

Say all five sentences to your partner.
Your partner will say *Question* or *Statement*.

A Look at the chart.

Adverbs of degree + adjectives	
What's she like?	She's **nice**. She's **very kind**. She's **not very interesting**. She's **sort of serious**.

B Write the number of the question next to the correct answer.

1. What's your father like?   _____ She's funny.
2. What are her parents like?   _____ It's boring.
3. What's Pete's new girlfriend like?   _____ He's nice.
4. What's your job like?   _____ They're friendly.

C Add an adverb to the answers in part B and write them in the spaces.

1. (really) _____
2. (extremely) _____
3. (kind of) _____
4. (very) _____

6 Talk Some More

A Write the expressions in the correct spaces.

(kind of serious)   (very funny)

   (really nice)   (really friendly)

Mario: So, how's the new job?
Norma: It's _____. I just met Larry. He seems _____.
Mario: Oh no! He's _____. He makes us laugh all the time!
Norma: Really? How about Jim, the mechanic?
Mario: He's _____.
Norma: Great! I think I'll go say 'hello.'

Spotlight

With adjectives which can be negative, like *serious* or *boring*, use *kind of* to make them sound softer.

B Check your answers.

Pair work

C Practice the conversation with a partner. Then practice again using different adjectives.

Work In Pairs (Student A)

A Think of a job for Tom, Rebecca and Shawn.

Write them here:

Tom is a(n) _____
Rebecca is a(n) _____
Shawn is a(n) _____

Tom	Rebecca	Shawn

- Doesn't smile very much.
- Always stays in the office until 9:00 pm.

- Likes helping other people.
- Tells great jokes.

- Always says hello.
- Usually leaves work early.

B You and your partner both started work in the same office recently. Use the information above to talk about the people you met there.

C What words would you use to describe the people above? Does your partner agree?

No, what's she like?

Did you meet Kim, the manager?

Try this

Think of a person in your class. Write your description. Then describe him/her to your partner. Your partner will guess who you are describing.

_____
_____
_____
_____

Work In Pairs   Student B

Student A: Use page 123

A Think of a job for Robert, Gina and Sandy.

Write them here:

Robert is a(n) _____

Gina is a(n) _____

Sandy is a(n) _____

Robert	**Gina**	**Sandy**

- Likes telling stories.
- Smiles and says hello every morning.

- Never says hello.
- Is always in front of the computer.

- Listens to other people.
- Always arrives at the office first.

B You and your partner both started work in the same office recently. Use the information above to talk about the people you met there.

C What words would you use to describe the people above? Does your partner agree?

Try this

Think of a person in your class. Write your description. Then describe him/her to your partner. Your partner will guess who you are describing.

_____

_____

_____

_____

Express Yourself

(A) How would you describe...

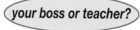
your boss or teacher?   your job or class?   your best friend?

learning English?   a brother or sister?   your daily life?

Use these words, or any others you know.

- *very*
- *really*
- *kind of*
- *not very*
- *funny*
- *hardworking*
- *nice*
- *friendly*
- *interesting*
- *serious*
- *boring*
- *smart*

 Group work

(B) Share your information with the other people in your group.

 Think About It

Don't judge a book by its cover.
This expression means that we can't always tell what someone is like by looking at them.

- Do you believe this is true?
- Do you have a similar expression in your language?

10 **Write About It**

(A) Look at this message.

(B) On a piece of paper, write to a friend or family member telling them about your English class, and the people you study with.

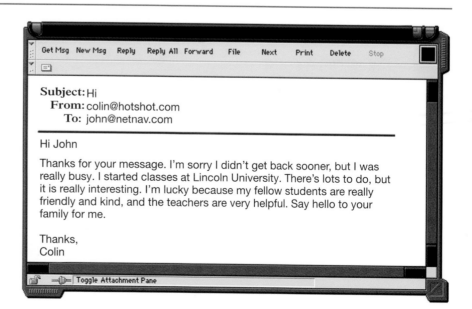

Get Msg   New Msg   Reply   Reply All   Forward   File   Next   Print   Delete   Stop

Subject: Hi
From: colin@hotshot.com
To: john@netnav.com

Hi John

Thanks for your message. I'm sorry I didn't get back sooner, but I was really busy. I started classes at Lincoln University. There's lots to do, but it is really interesting. I'm lucky because my fellow students are really friendly and kind, and the teachers are very helpful. Say hello to your family for me.

Thanks,
Colin

Toggle Attachment Pane

• Strategy: Inferring vocabulary

How important is personality in a business partnership?

Amy Nelson, Police Officer

My partner just got promoted, so I'm getting a new person soon. In my business, my life sometimes depends on my partner. I need someone who is always paying attention to what's happening around us. A good police officer must really understand human nature.

Sarah Freeland, Caterer

I provide the food for parties and banquets. My business has grown a lot, and I'm looking for a partner. I need someone who can do several things at the same time. My partner must show up for work on time and work long hours. I need someone who can work fast, and will never be impolite to our customers.

Jonathan Mead, Resort Owner

I own a little resort in the mountains. I have five cabins on a lake. I advertise, rent the cabins, clean them, rent boats, and operate a little store. I'm looking for a new partner now because my current partner is getting married. I need someone who really likes people, who doesn't lose his temper, and who loves nature.

Find words in the text that mean the same as:

Paragraph 1

1. got a better job   (2 words)   _____

2. the way people think and act   (2 words)   _____

Paragraph 2

3. many   (1 word)   _____

4. rude or bad mannered   (1 word)   _____

Paragraph 3

5. present   (1 word)   _____

6. get angry   (3 words)   _____

Talk About It

- What kind of person are you? Describe your personality.
- What kind of job do you think is good for someone with your personality? Why?
- What kind of job do you think is not suitable for someone with your personality? Why?

12 Review

1 Vocabulary Review

A Fill in the chart with adjectives you learned in this unit.

Positive Adjectives	Negative Adjectives	Positive or Negative Adjectives
_____	_____	_____
_____	_____	_____
_____	_____	_____
_____	_____	_____

B Which of these words describe *you*?

What's the new teacher like?

2 Grammar Review

A Fill in the blanks.

1. _____ you meet the new boss?   Yes, I _____ .
2. _____ she like?   _____ very friendly.
3. _____ you meet the new designer?   No, I _____ .
4. _____ he like?   _____ very hardworking.
5. _____ you meet the new mechanic? No, I _____ .
6. _____ he like?   _____ extremely funny.

B Make up sentences using the words shown.

1. (kind of/doctor/serious)   *The new doctor is kind of serious.*
2. (cashier/really/interesting)   _____
3. (kind of/manager/boring)   _____
4. (pump attendant/funny/very)   _____
5. (smart/extremely/teacher)   _____

3 Log On

Practice more with the language and topics you studied on the *Expressions* website:

http://expressions.heinle.com

UNIT 16

Goals

○ *Talking about what you did*　　○ *Asking about past events*

I lost my cell phone.

1 Get Ready

A What did Greg
do today?
Write the number
next to the correct
picture (1–5).

> 1. Took out some money
> 2. Picked up shirts
> 3. Worked out
> 4. Had lunch with Cindy
> 5. Bought flowers for Mom

 Pair work

B Work with a partner and make up one more activity for each place Greg went today.

2 Start Talking 🎞

A Look at the conversation and listen.

> Greg: Oh, no! I lost my cell phone.
> Pete: Oh, that's terrible, Greg! Where did you go today?
> Greg: Well, first, I went to the dry cleaners. Then, I went
> to the bank. Next, I had lunch with my girlfriend...

 Pair work

B Practice the conversation with a partner. Practice again,
but extend the conversation to talk about everything Greg did today.

3 Listen In

A Look at the activities below. Where do people do these things?

> • picked up a credit card   • bought chocolates   • picked up shirts
>
> • bought flowers   • had pizza   • bought workout clothes   • had a hamburger
>
> • picked up pants   • picked up an ATM card   • worked out at the gym

B Listen and circle the things Greg did.

C Listen again and number the places in the order you hear them (1–5).

4 Say It Right

A Circle the word with the different vowel sound in each group.

1.	lost	bought	saw	shut
2.	picked up	went	said	left
3.	lay	ate	called	made
4.	put	found	took	looked

Try this

Add one more word to each line in the exercise. There will be one word left. Which one?

paid   read   spoke
cooked   brought

B Listen and check your answers.

C Listen again and practice.

5 Focus In

A Look at the chart.

Simple past	
How **was** your day?	It **was** busy.
What **did** you do today?	First, I **went** to the bank.
	Then, I **picked** up my cleaning.
	Next, I **had** lunch with my boyfriend.
	Finally, I **studied** for my test.

B Write the correct past verb forms in the spaces.

go _____ have _____ pick _____
is _____ work _____ make _____
are _____ study _____ put _____
do _____ buy _____ read _____

C Think of four things you did yesterday. Write sentences in the blanks.

First, I got up and _____.
Then, _____.
Next, _____.
Finally, _____.

6 Talk Some More

A Fill in the missing information.

Pete: So, Greg, how was your day?
Greg: It was busy. I went to the bank.
Pete: What for?
Greg: _____. Then I went to the fitness center.
Pete: What did you do there?
Greg: _____.
Pete: Uh huh.
Greg: And then I went to Rosie's Grill for lunch.
Pete: Who did you have lunch with?
Greg: _____.

B Check your answers.

Pair work **C** Practice the conversation with a partner.
Practice again using information about your own day.

Work In Pairs   (Student A)

A Write the words and expressions in the correct order below.

(tomorrow)   (the day before yesterday)   (the day after tomorrow)   (yesterday)

_____, _____, today, _____, _____

B Ask your partner questions. Note what the people did and who they saw yesterday.

NAME	WENT	SAW
Pete	office, the movies	
Sandy		friends, family
Bill	gym, school	
Gina		cashier, doctor, nurse

C Answer your partner's questions about the people in the chart.

Where did you go today?

Well, first I went to the office...

Try this

Now ask your partner about his/her day. Get as much information as you can and write it here. Note the things your partner did in the correct order.

_____
_____
_____
_____

Work In Pairs Student B

Student A: Use page 131

(A) Write the words and expressions in the correct order below.

tomorrow

the day before yesterday

the day after tomorrow

yesterday

_____, _____, today, _____, _____

(B) Answer your partner's questions about the people in the chart.

NAME	WENT	SAW
Pete		boss, secretary, co-workers
Sandy	birthday party, lunch at Mom's	
Bill		instructor, teachers, students
Gina	supermarket, medical center	

(C) Ask your partner questions. Note what the people did and who they saw yesterday.

Where did you go today?

Well, first I went to the office...

Try this

Now ask your partner about his/her day. Get as much information as you can and write it here. Note the things your partner did in the correct order.

_____

_____

_____

_____

8 Express Yourself

A Make a list of the places you went and the people you talked to last weekend.

Places I went

_____

_____

_____

_____

_____

People I saw

_____

_____

_____

_____

_____

Group work **B** Take turns asking and answering about the places you went and the people you saw. Who in the group had the most interesting weekend?

And where did you go yesterday?

9 *Think About It*

People say the world is getting smaller. Our social networks are changing. In these days of e-mail and cell phones, although we talk to more people, we see them less.

- What do you think about this trend? Do you think it will continue?
- Do you like using cell phones and e-mail? Why or why not?

10 Write About It

A Look at the diary entry.

B Now write a diary entry about what you did yesterday.

Dear Diary,

_____

_____

Dear Diary,
Today was a beautiful, sunny day. At the end of class in the morning, I had lunch in a cafe with some of my classmates. In the afternoon I studied, and then I went to the fitness center and worked out. Around six o'clock my friend Mike phoned and invited me to go see a movie. It was a science fiction movie and it was really exciting. After the movie we went to an Italian restaurant for pizza. What a great day!

11 Read On   The Unclaimed Baggage Store

• **Strategy: Identifying reference words**

Did you ever lose something on an airplane trip?
Did you wonder what happened to it?

Every year travelers lose things on airplanes. In 1970, a man and a woman had a great idea for a business. They bought unclaimed lost items from the airlines. Then they sold them in their store in Scottsboro, Alabama, U.S.A. They named the store 'Unclaimed Baggage.'

There's nothing like this store, and the prices are great. Shoppers can buy used clothing, cameras, jewelry, glasses, electronics, sporting goods, and books. Of course, they can buy lots of used suitcases too!

Sometimes the store owners buy strange things. They have no idea what they are, so they put pictures of them on their website. If you can identify one of these things, they will send you a free 'Unclaimed Baggage' T-shirt.

When you buy something from them, it's yours. So a woman was very surprised when her little girl pulled the head off of a Barbie doll that she bought there. Inside the body they found $500.

Some things are sold online. But the best place to buy is at the store itself, which is very large. If you're ever in Alabama, you should go there. You might find something you lost!

Look at these sentences from the reading passage.
What does the underlined word mean in each one?

1. They bought unclaimed lost items from the airlines.   The man and woman
2. Of course, they can buy lots of used suitcases, too. _____
3. They have no idea what they are. _____
4. Inside the body they found $500. _____
5. If you're ever in Alabama, you should go there. _____

Talk About It

○ Have you ever lost something on a trip? What and where?

○ Have you ever found something interesting? What and where?

○ Do you think that a store like this would be popular in your country? Why or why not?

①　Vocabulary Review

Ⓐ Fill in the chart with the verbs you learned in this unit.

Regular Verbs	Irregular Verbs
_____ _____	_____ _____
_____ _____	_____ _____
_____ _____	_____ _____
_____ _____	_____ _____

Ⓑ Can you add any more verbs to the two columns?

②　Grammar Review

Ⓐ Fill in the blanks in the conversation.

A: How _____ your day?

B: Busy. I _____ to the fitness center.

and _____ out hard.

A: What _____ you _____ next?

B: I _____ lunch with my friend.

We _____ to Colin's Café.

A: What _____ you _____?

B: A hamburger and french fries.

I lost my glasses!

That's too bad!

Ⓑ Write four sentences about what you did yesterday.

1. _____

2. _____

3. _____

4. _____

③　Log On

Practice more with the language and topics you studied on the *Expressions* website:

http://expressions.heinle.com

UNIT 1   Language Summary   *Are you Dr. Lowe?*

Am I in the right class?	Yes, you are.
	No, you aren't. You're in Class B.
Are you Pat?	Yes, I am.
	No, I'm not. I'm Peggy.
Is he/she Pat?	Yes, he/she is.
	No, he/she isn't.
Are they sisters?	Yes, they are.
	No, they aren't. They're friends.

What's	your	name?		My	name is...
	his			His	
	her			Her	

○ WORD BUILDER
Write down any new words from this unit you want to remember.

UNIT 2   Language Summary   *Is that your family?*

Is	this	your family?	Yes, it is.
	that	your husband?	No, it isn't.
Are	these	your children?	Yes, they are.
	those	your parents?	No, they aren't.

Do you have any brothers or sisters?	Yes, I do.
	No, I don't.
	I have one brother and two sisters.

○ WORD BUILDER
Write down any new words from this unit you want to remember.

Do you know Amy?	Yes, I do.
	Yes, I know her.
	No, I don't.
	No, I don't know her.

Does he/she have short hair?	Yes, he/she does.
	No, he/she doesn't.
	No, he/she has long hair.

| Is he/she tall? | Yes, he/she is. |
| | No, he/she isn't. |

| What does he/she look like? | He/She's | tall. |
| | He/She has | blond hair. |

○ **WORD BUILDER**
Write down any new words from this unit you want to remember.

Where are you from?	I'm from Mexico.
Where do you come from?	I come from Mexico.
Where is he/she from?	He's/she's from Canada.
Where does he/she come from?	He/she comes from Canada.

| What do you do? | I'm a teacher. |
| Where do you live? | I live in Singapore. |

○ **WORD BUILDER**
Write down any new words from this unit you want to remember.

Make yourself at home.

Come in. Make yourself at home.	Thank you. Thanks a lot.

Would you like some juice?	Yes, please. No, thank you.
Would you like orange or apple juice?	Apple, please.

May I have some water?	Sure. Here you are.

○ *WORD BUILDER*
Write down any new words from this unit you want to remember.

How much is this sweater?

How much	is this sweater? is it?	It's $16.
	are the shoes? are they?	They're $79.

How many T-shirts do you need?	One.
How many pairs of shoes do you need?	I need two pairs.

I'll take this shirt.	That'll be $30, please.

Do you take credit cards?	Yes, we do. No, we don't.

○ *WORD BUILDER*
Write down any new words from this unit you want to remember.

Is there a pool?

Excuse me.	Yes, sir? Yes, ma'am?

Is there a business center in this hotel?	Yes, there is. No, there isn't.

Where is it?	It's on the second floor. It's next to the coffee shop. It's between the pool and the health club.

How do I get there?	Take the stairs to the second floor. It's next to the health club.

○ **WORD BUILDER**
Write down any new words from
this unit you want to remember.

First, you turn it on.

Do you know how to use a computer?	Yes, it's easy. No, it looks difficult.

Do you know how to use a VCR? I can't turn on the VCR.	First, you need to plug it in. Then, you have to press the *on* button. Finally, press the *play* button.

○ **WORD BUILDER**
Write down any new words from
this unit you want to remember.

| What's the matter? | I'm tired. |

| Why are you tired?
How come? | I get up at 5:30 every morning.
I have an early morning class. |

What do you do in the morning?	I go to school.
What time do they study in the afternoon?	They study at 3:00.
What does she do in the afternoon?	She reads the newspaper.
What does he do at night?	He watches TV.

○ **WORD BUILDER**
Write down any new words from this unit you want to remember.

UNIT 10 *Language Summary* *I'd like a hamburger.*

| Can I help you? | Yes, I'd like a hamburger, please.
No, thanks. |

| What size would you like? | Medium, please.
I'll have a medium, please. |

| Would you like ketchup and mustard on that? | Yes, please.
I'll have some ketchup, but I don't want any mustard.
No, thank you. |

| Is that all? | Yes, thanks. |
| | No, I'll have an iced tea. |

○ **WORD BUILDER**
Write down any new words from this unit you want to remember.

| What are you doing tonight? | I'm going to a concert. |
| What's Pete up to this evening? | He has to work late. |

Do you want to see a movie?	What's playing?
	Which one?
Do you want to go to a concert?	Who's playing?

Do you want to see a movie tonight?	That sounds good.
How about seeing a movie tonight?	I'd love to.
	Sorry, I'm going to a party tonight.
	Oh, no. I have to work tonight.

○ WORD BUILDER
Write down any new words from this unit you want to remember.

| What's the weather like? | It's hot and sunny. |
| What's the weather going to be like? | It's going to be cloudy. |

Let's go on a picnic.	OK. That sounds like a good idea.
	I don't think it's a good idea. It's going to rain tomorrow.
What are you going to do on the weekend?	I'm not sure. Maybe I'll play tennis.

○ WORD BUILDER
Write down any new words from this unit you want to remember.

What can we get him?

What do you like?	I like painting.
What does he/she like doing?	He/She likes playing tennis.

What can we get him/her?	Let's get him/her a CD.	Great idea. I'm sure he'll/she'll like that.
	How about getting him/her a CD?	No, he/she already has a lot of CDs.

○ WORD BUILDER
Write down any new words from this unit you want to remember.

We should go to the beach.

Can you swim?	Yes, I can. No, I can't.
Can Mario speak English?	Yes, he can. No, he can't.

Where should we go on vacation?	I think we should go to the beach.

What can we do at the beach?	We can go windsurfing.

We should go to the mountains.	But I don't like hiking.

○ WORD BUILDER
Write down any new words from this unit you want to remember.

UNIT 15 Language Summary   *What's she like?*

Did you meet the new cashier?	Yes, I did.
	No, I didn't.

What's he/she like?	He's/She's	extremely very really	nice interesting boring
How's your new job?	It's	kind of sort of not very	

○ WORD BUILDER
Write down any new words from this unit you want to remember.

- ○ _____
- ○ _____
- ○ _____
- ○ _____
- ○ _____
- ○ _____

UNIT 16 Language Summary   *I lost my cell phone.*

I lost my wallet.	That's terrible!

How was your day?	It was busy.
What did you do?	First, I ate breakfast. Then, I went to school. Next, I did my homework in the library. Finally, I met some friends and we had dinner.

○ WORD BUILDER
Write down any new words from this unit you want to remember.

- ○ _____
- ○ _____
- ○ _____
- ○ _____
- ○ _____
- ○ _____

Congratulations! *You've finished Book 1.*

A What did you enjoy about *Expressions*?

○ Check (✔) the boxes.

	Not at all	A little	A lot
I enjoyed the speaking activities.			
I enjoyed the listening activities.			
I enjoyed the reading activities.			
I enjoyed the writing activities.			
I enjoyed the grammar activities.			
I enjoyed the vocabulary activities.			
I am now a better English learner.			

B Preferences

○ Which were the most useful for improving your English? Put them in order (1–6).

_____ Working on my own   _____ Role plays

_____ Pair work   _____ Review activities

_____ Group work   _____ Internet activities

C Assess

○ Now look back at the chart on page 7. Are any of your choices different now? How?

○ How will you continue to improve your English? Write down four ideas.

Good luck with your continued English studies!